COMPETITION AND INTELLECTUAL PROPERTY RIGHTS

ORGANISATION FOR ECONOMIC CO-OPERATION AND DEVELOPMENT

Pursuant to article 1 of the Convention signed in Paris on 14th December 1960, and which came into force on 30th September 1961, the Organisation for Economic Co-operation and Development (OECD) shall promote policies designed:

- to achieve the highest sustainable economic growth and employment and a rising standard of living in Member countries, while maintaining financial stability, and thus to contribute to the development of the world economy;
- to contribute to sound economic expansion in Member as well as non-member countries in the process of economic development; and
- to contribute to the expansion of world trade on a multilateral, non-discriminatory basis in accordance with international obligations.

The original Member countries of the OECD are Austria, Belgium, Canada, Denmark, France, the Federal Republic of Germany, Greece, Iceland, Ireland, Italy, Luxembourg, the Netherlands, Norway, Portugal, Spain, Sweden, Switzerland, Turkey, the United Kingdom and the United States. The following countries acceded subsequently through accession at the dates indicated hereafter: Japan (28th April 1964), Finland (28th January 1969), Australia (7th June 1971) and New Zealand (29th May 1973).

The Socialist Federal Republic of Yugoslavia takes part in some of the work of the OECD (agreement of 28th October 1961).

Publié en français sous le titre:

POLITIQUE DE CONCURRENCE
ET PROPRIÉTÉ INTELLECTUELLE

Intellectual property licensing is a challenging topic for competition authorities. The licensing of intellectual property benefits the competitive process by diffusing innovation and by helping innovators to capture their rewards, thereby increasing the incentives to others to try to innovate as well. However, licensing agreements can also serve to cartelize an industry or to increase the market power of a single licensor. The problem for competition authorities is to determine whether a particular agreement is likely to help or hurt competition. The problem is particulary difficult as a restrictive clause in a licensing agreement may be either pro- or anticompetitive, depending on the circumstances.

This report presents a comprehensive analysis of the various competitive effects of restrictions in licensing agreements and suggests how such agreements should be handled by competition authorities. In the course of this review, the report describes the relevant competition laws and policies of OECD Member countries and provides a critical analysis of relevant case law and administrative decisions. Included in the report is a summary of recent (1988 and 1989) regulations and enforcement guidelines published by the Japanese Fair Trade Commission, the United States Department of Justice and the Commission of the European Communities.

Also available

PREDATORY PRICING (May 1989)
(24 89 02 1) ISBN 92-64-13245-7   110 pages   £8.50   US$15.00   FF70.00   DM29.00

DEREGULATION AND AIRLINE COMPETITION (June 1988)
(24 88 02 1) ISBN 92-64-13101-9   168 pages   £12.00   US$22.00   FF100.00   DM43.00

INTERNATIONAL MERGERS AND COMPETITION POLICY (December 1988) bilingual
(24 88 03 3) ISBN 92-64-03143-X   115 pages   £11.00   US$20.00   FF90.00   DM39.00

THE COSTS OF RESTRICTING IMPORTS: The Automobile Industry (January 1988)
(24 87 06 1) ISBN 92-64-13037-3   174 pages   £8.50   US$18.00   FF85.00   DM36.00

COMPETITION POLICY AND JOINT VENTURES (February 1987)
(24 86 03 1) ISBN 92-64-12898-0   112 pages   £6.50   US$13.00   FF65.00   DM29.00

COMPETITION POLICY IN OECD COUNTRIES:

   1987-1988 (February 1989)
   (24 89 01 1) ISBN 92-64-13192-2   294 pages   £19.50   US$34.00   FF160.00   DM66.00

   1986-1987 (May 1988)
   (24 88 01 1) ISBN 92-64-13075-6   284 pages   £15.00   US$27.50   FF125.00   DM54.00

   1985-1986 (October 1987)
   (24 87 04 1) ISBN 92-64-12970-7   272 pages   £8.00   US$17.00   FF80.00   DM34.00

COMPETITION POLICY AND THE PROFESSIONS (February 1985)
(24 85 01 1) ISBN 92-64-12685-6   112 pages   £7.50   US$15.00   FF75.00   DM33.00

MERGER POLICIES AND RECENT TRENDS IN MERGERS (October 1984)
(24 84 06 1) ISBN 92-64-12624-4   122 pages   £6.30   US$13.00   FF63.00   DM28.00

COMPETITION AND TRADE POLICIES. Their Interaction (October 1984)
(24 84 05 1) ISBN 92-64-12625-2   154 pages   £6.00   US$12.00   FF60.00   DM27.00

COMPETITION LAW ENFORCEMENT. International Co-operation in the Collection of Information (March 1984)
(24 84 01 1) ISBN 92-64-12553-1   126 pages   £6.00   US$12.00   FF60.00   DM27.00

Prices charged at the OECD Bookshop.

*THE OECD CATALOGUE OF PUBLICATIONS and supplements will be sent free of charge
on request addressed either to OECD Publications Service,
2, rue André-Pascal, 75775 PARIS CEDEX 16, or to the OECD Distributor in your country.*

TABLE OF CONTENTS

Chapter 1

INTRODUCTION

The growth of new technologies in recent years is a phenomenon which poses challenges and opportunities across many disciplines. These new advances, for example in information and communications technologies, in biotechnology and in the development of new materials, may provide an important impetus to re-igniting economic growth across the OECD as scientific advance is an important component in the promotion of economic growth[1].

A variety of Committees within the OECD are presently working to analyse and interpret the process of technological change and its economic, social and international implications. The concerns currently being dealt with by various Committees include the role of government policy for innovation and diffusion of technology; the economic impact of new technologies; the risks of new technologies; and international competition and co-operation in technology. Competition policy can play an important role in a number of the factors outlined above. In particular, competition policy may affect certain incentives to create new technology, may affect the way new technology is diffused throughout a national economy and internationally, and guards against certain risks to competition which stem from restrictive business practices involving the licensing of technology.

Competition policy may affect incentives to create new technology in three main ways. First, competition policy in many Member countries guards against the creation of excessive concentration and market power through merger control. This is significant in that incentives to innovate are believed to be greater when an industry is not monopolized. Perfect competition, however, may also reduce the incentives to invest in R & D, leading some writers to argue that intermediate levels of concentration are most conducive to successful R & D[2]. A second major aspect of the interaction between competition policy and innovation concerns the application of competition rules to research and development joint ventures. A recent Report by this Committee noted the particular benefits of R & D joint ventures - cost-sharing, risk-spreading and reducing free-rider problems and duplicative research - and, in its suggestions to national authorities, noted that R & D joint ventures, apart from certain special circumstances, generally do not raise competitive concerns[3]. The last major element, and the subject of the present Report, concerns the relationship between competition policy and the licensing of intellectual property rights.

The manner in which competition policy is applied to the licensing of intellectual property can have an important influence on the creation of new technology. First, competition policy may affect directly the profitability of innovation. Increasing the potential profits which can be derived from technical innovation will generally increase investments in R & D. Part of those profits are obtained through the licensing of technology usually

7

protected from appropriation by intellectual property rights, to other users. To the extent that the application of competition laws and policies to licensing agreements affects the actual or anticipated returns to innovation, the incentive to create and diffuse new technology may be affected. Second, the regulation of technology licensing through competition law and policy may indirectly affect the incentives to innovate by influencing the structure of the market for technology.

Given the importance of innovation to growth, care should be exercised so that competition law enforcement does not hamper the creation and diffusion of innovations. However, competition authorities cannot simply adopt a permissive policy as patent and know-how licensing agreements can lead to serious cartel problems, including price fixing, output restrictions and market and customer divisions. The object of this Report is to find the correct balance which satisfies all of these concerns.

The most recent work by the Committee in the patent area is the 1972 Report on Restrictive Business Practices and Patent Licensing Agreements which led to a 1974 Council Recommendation on Patents and Licences[4]. That Recommendation focused largely on the anticompetitive consequences thought to result from various licensing practices, such as fixing resale prices, granting exclusive territories, limiting output, restricting fields of use and tying requirements. Since that time, however, there have been a number of developments which made a review of that work appropriate. First, a number of Member countries have introduced new competition rules or amended existing ones since the 1972 Report. Some of these new rules deal specifically with intellectual property issues. Second, fresh thinking has been applied by competition authorities, courts and legal and economic writers to even longstanding types of intellectual property licensing practices. This new thinking can be traced to several developments. One is a growing appreciation of the existence of competition between technologies which are economic substitutes. Another is a growing consensus on the economic consequences of vertical restraints, an analysis which can be applied directly to the licensing of intellectual property. Third, experience has been gained with various remedies applied to correct patent abuses. Finally, whole new areas of technology have emerged since the last report, creating new and possibly difficult factual settings for the application of competition policy. This latter area includes such diverse areas as biotechnology and integrated circuits.

In light of these concerns the Committee on Competition Law and Policy created this Working Party under the following mandate:

    a)   To study and report to the Committee on the relationship between competition law and policy and intellectual property rights, in particular patents, know-how and related licensing agreements, taking into account work on intellecutal property rights in other parts of the Organisation and other international fora;

    b)   In the light of the findings of the study to make appropriate policy recommendations relating, inter alia, to the 1974 Recommendation on patents and licenses.

The earlier Report and Recommendation focused on patent licensing practices without taking into consideration the issues related to the licensing of know-how. The omission of know-how practices is a shortcoming of the earlier work given the importance of agreements involving either pure know-how or a mixture of patents and know-how. Some competition policy authorities believe that firms are increasingly keeping their intellectual property in the form of know-how rather than seeking patent protection, citing the costs and delays in obtaining patents, the lengthy litigation which can accompany a patent application and the weak protection afforded by the patent laws of some developing countries. Pure know-how licensing agreements, however, are still less common than agreements involving only patents or both patents and know-how[5].

When examining know-how licensing it is important to keep in mind that know-how differs from patent-protected intellectual property in a number of important ways. Patents, of course, are created by law, have a fixed term and geographic effect and are public, all in sharp contrast to the amorphous, indefinite and private nature of know-how. Further, a patent, being a property right, includes the right to exclude others from unauthorized use of the innovation while know-how can be independently discovered and used, placing a premium on secrecy. One goal of this report will be to identify what implications, if any, these legal and practical differences have for the competitive consequences of patent and know-how licensing. To the extent that no significant differences appear, the report will treat the two interchangeably. At times, however, the analyses will diverge. These areas are identified in the chapters which follow.

The goal of this Report then is to provide a thorough review of competition policy regulation of intellectual property licensing agreements. The next two chapters of this report develop the inter-relationships between the licensing of intellectual property and competition policy, setting forth the particular procompetitive rationales for various licensing provisions and the areas of clear concern to competition policy. Chapter IV will describe the competition law and policy provisions applicable to these agreements, including statutes and regulations. Chapter V will summarize current enforcement policies in Member countries, including judicial trends and positions taken by enforcement officials. The final Chapter will summarize the main lessons of the exercise and provide a suggested structure for the review of licensing agreements by enforcement officials.

Chapter 2

COMPETITION POLICY
AND INTELLECTUAL PROPERTY RIGHTS

Intellectual property rights are designed to promote the creation of innovations and thus to promote economic advance and consumer welfare. This occurs by giving the innovator an exclusive legal right to the economic exploitation of his innovation for a period of time; the reaping of profits serves both to reward the innovator for his investment and to induce others to strive to innovate in the future. If innovators were not granted property rights in their work, widespread copying could be expected to occur, diminishing the returns to the innovator and the incentive to innovate[1]. Thus, the ability to exclude imitation is the most important aspect of the property rights granted to the innovator. Intellectual property rights also include the right to license others to exploit the innovation. Licensing is an important additional source of income to the innovator, and can be the only source when the holder of the property right is not well situated to engage in large scale commercial exploitation[2].

Competition policy seeks to promote consumer welfare by removing impediments to the efficient functioning of markets. This is accomplished by preventing cartels aimed at price fixing, limiting output or otherwise restricting competition, by preventing firms from gaining market power in unjustified ways, e.g. through anticompetitive mergers with competitors, by raising the barriers to entry facing new firms, and by preventing firms with market power from abusing their dominant positions. Although intellectual property licensing agreements are generally procompetitive, they may be anticompetitive where they are a mere sham for a cartel arrangement, where they restrict competition between technologies that are economic substitutes for one another or where they exclude new technologies from the market.

The goals of competition policy described above are generally associated with efforts to promote short run allocative efficiency, that is, efforts which tend to drive prices toward marginal cost which in turn maximizes the output of society's resources[3]. This general thrust may appear to be in conflict with the exclusionary rights embodied in intellectual property rights. That is, an innovation (i.e., intellectual property) is essentially information which has a zero marginal cost of use, i.e. a given piece of information can be used by an infinite number of people simultaneously and without exhausting the information itself. Thus, the right to exclude allows positive prices to be charged for use of the information and tends to restrict output (or more accurately dissemination of the information). This apparent conflict can be reconciled if consumer welfare is viewed in the long run. That is, long-run consumer welfare depends on the dynamic efficiency of the economy as well as its tendency towards allocative efficiency. Dynamic efficiency includes the invention and commercial introduction of new products and processes which enhance welfare both by increasing the quality of goods and by promoting growth through increased productive efficiency[4]. The goals of competition policy

11

include these aspects of dynamic efficiency and some competition statutes include them explicitly in the factors to be taken into account by competition authorities.

It should also be kept in mind that patents simply create property rights. Property rights, of course, are the cornerstone of any efficient market economy. Rights in intellectual property are no different from rights in tangible assets in that they permit the exclusion of others from use of the asset. Thus, rights in intellectual property if properly used complement rather than conflict with the purposes of competition policy.

Innovations largely stem from investments in research and development and there is a direct positive correlation between R & D activity and innovative output[5]. Further, investment in R & D and innovative output have been shown to follow profit opportunities[6]. As potential profits rise, investments in R & D can be expected to rise as well[7]. Thus, to gain the innovation necessary for dynamic efficiency the innovator must be able to anticipate receiving a sufficient return on his investment within the often short commercial life of the innovation.

Intellectual property rights protection also reduces the cost of transmitting innovations. By defining the nature of the protection (e.g., the innovator's right to exclude) and the scope of the protection (e.g., the description of the innovation protected), intellectual property rights provide the legal building blocks that enable the owner of an innovation to license the innovation to others. For example, patent protection enables a patentee to disclose its innovation, without fear of copying, to potential licensees in order to enable them to evaluate the value of the innovation. Such disclosure increases certainty, decreases risk, and so reduces the cost of licence transactions.

Accepting the need to reward innovation implies that the innovator is allowed to price that innovation higher than its marginal cost. That is, an innovation, *once created*, comes close to being a free good. Repeated use does not exhaust an innovation. But pricing at marginal cost, while promoting maximum allocative and productive efficiency in the present, would likely reduce the supply of innovations in the future[8].

The key question here is how much reward is necessary to bring forward "enough" innovation. Some commentators believe that, in a number of industries at least, market conditions are such that innovation would occur even without the exclusive patent right and attendant allocative inefficiencies. A number of factors have been identified, including the "first mover" advantage and fear of losing market share to competitors who innovate[9].

How competition policy authorities treat the question of reward-for-innovation is crucial in determining how to analyse the competitive effects of intellectual property licensing practices. For example, if one believes that "enough" innovation would occur without intellectual property rights or, alternatively, that competition authorities should be concerned exclusively with allocative efficiency then one takes a quite different view of the competitive effects of licensing practices than if one believes that permitting innovators to fully appropriate their surpluses is procompetitive. This report, however, does not attempt to balance the loss in dynamic efficiency from lost innovation against the gain in static efficiency from reducing unnecessary rewards to innovators. It is not within the scope of this report to define what level of reward is sufficient to call for "enough" innovation; that is done by laws governing the scope and duration of intellectual property rights. The focus of the report rather is on the competitive effects of intellectual property licensing agreements.

Competition policy affects the use of intellectual property rights in two main ways. First, and most importantly, competition policy applies to the clauses used in agreements to license inventions. Second, competition policy may impose certain remedies for abuses, compulsory licensing in particular, which affects the innovator immediately and can alter future behaviour as well.

The decisions which competition policy authorities take with respect to acceptable intellectual property licensing agreements are of more than academic interest; the licensing activities of firms are routinely affected. Some suggestion of this impact can be found in the views of licensing executives. While the self-interest of these executives is clear, their responses do suggest that competition policy in OECD countries plays a significant role in firms' licensing practices. According to a recent survey of such executives conducted by the OECD, competition policy is seen by those licensors as the most important disincentive to licensing activities in OECD countries[10].

An earlier study of United States firms involved in international technology licensing sheds some additional light on their practices, showing that firms commonly seek to impose restrictions on non-affiliated licensees. There are limits, however, in what one can conclude from Table 1, in particular from the finding that price, quantity, exclusivity and tie-in provisions are sought relatively infrequently. This could mean that such terms are relatively unimportant to licensors. It seems possible, however, that the treatment such provisions receive under competition laws is reflected in licensor behaviour[11].

Table 1[12].
Restrictions sought in agreements

Restrictions	Percentage of responding licensor firms
Territorial limitation on manufacture	82.4
Limitations on licensee's export quantity	14.7
Limitations on licencee's export price	5.9
Export only through designated agent	23.5
Prohibition handling competitor's products	23.5
Materials to be purchased from licencors or designated agents	11.8
Grantbacks from licensees	70.6
Quality controls on materials	29.4
Quality controls on finished product	55.9

The remedies which competition policy officials apply to violators also can have important consequences on future behaviour. The excessive use of compulsory licensing, for example, could lead to increased secrecy and lower investment in R & D[13]. Scherer has studied the impact of United States compulsory licensing decrees on subsequent investments in R & D and patenting practices of the companies involved[14]. He found that firms subject to mandatory licensing decrees did not, perhaps surprisingly, reduce their subsequent investments in R & D relative to their competitors R & D efforts[15]. On the other hand, when he examined patenting activities of firms before and after the imposition of compulsory licensing decrees, he found that patenting dropped substantially in the post-decree period and that the drop was steepest for those firms required to do the most licensing[16]. This is significant in that to the extent that innovations are held in the form of secret know-how rather than as patents, their diffusion is likely to be restricted. This stems from the fact that pure know-how agreements are likely to be more difficult to negotiate than mixed patent and know-how agreements.

13

What can be concluded from these studies is that firms with technology to license feel themselves to be constrained by competition policy. This perception is reflected in the restrictions which they seek in their licensing agreements.

Chapter 3

A SUMMARY OF COMPETITIVE EFFECTS

The preceding section described how competition policy affects patenting and licensing behaviour. Given that effect, it is important that the regulation of patent licensing agreements have a sound basis in economic analysis. This basis follows from an understanding of the nature and economic effects of intellectual property rights and related licensing agreements. From a competition perspective it will be necessary to identify and balance the possible pro- and anticompetitive effects rather than taking an overly general approach. This Chapter therefore presents a number of points concerning likely procompetitive effects of licensing agreements as well as the major possible anticompetitive effects. These two types of effects are presented separately in an effort to identify them more clearly. Thus when considering the procompetitive effect of a particular type of agreement, it would be useful to keep in mind that possibly serious anticompetitive effects will not be identified until later in the Chapter.

The competitive effects discussed in this chapter are concerned with the concept of market power. Preliminary issues are whether the granting of an exclusive right in intellectual property necessarily creates market power and whether whatever market power which is created can be "extended" or "leveraged" into additional market power in either the same or other markets. The chapter then turns to the question of possible pro- and anti-competitive effects of licensing restrictions. The procompetitive effects will generally not operate to increase the market power inherent in the innovation although they should increase the returns to the innovator. That is, these provisions can be thought of as corresponding to efforts by the innovator to capture more of the surplus created by the innovation. These procompetitive effects will generally correspond with restraints which operate vertically. Anticompetitive restraints, on the other hand, will be seen generally to operate in a horizontal fashion by outright cartelization, facilitating collusion or anticompetitively excluding entry in a market. Thus these latter practices serve to increase market power rather than to capture whatever value is inherent in an innovation.

The discussion of pro- and anticompetitive effects in this chapter will show that many clauses in licensing agreements can operate either to promote competition or to create a cartel. The effect will depend on the economic context of the agreement. This distinction will be important to keep in mind in later chapters, as it will be seen that competition policy in the past has often been guided solely by the type of clause used rather than on a total analysis of its economic effect in a given context. And, as discussed below, that economic effect will often hinge on whether the restrictive clause is used in a horizontal or vertical agreement.

A. LIMITS ON THE MARKET POWER
OF INTELLECTUAL PROPERTY RIGHTS (IPRs)

1. *IPRs and economic monopoly*

At least some of the uneasiness of competition policy with respect to IPRs can be traced to the notion that the creation of an IPR conveys an economic monopoly along with its bundle of exclusive legal rights. The belief is certainly not fanciful; numerous patents are, for example, extremely valuable. One routinely hears of new patented goods having projected sales of hundreds of millions of dollars. Likewise, everyday experience shows the economic power in copyrighted goods, witness, e.g., the fortunes made by some software producers or the box office receipts of certain films[1].

Thus, it is not surprising if courts and competition policy authorities associate intellectual property rights with economic power. This development is not a recent one in some Member countries. In the United States, for example, a series of Supreme Court decisions over the first half of this century resulted by 1947 in a rule which presumed market power when a tie-in practice involved a patented tying good[2]. By 1962 United States courts presumed market power to be present in tying cases involving either patented or copyrighted goods[3].

The creation of exclusive legal rights, however, does not necessarily establish the ability to exercise market power. This is as true with respect to intellectual property as it is for physical property. Property rights generally create exclusivity but market power stems from the nature of the demand for the property. This demand depends in turn on the availability of substitutes and the cross-elasticity of demand between these possible substitutes, and also on cross-elasticity of demand between the patented item and complementary goods[4]. As one commentator has stated, "a patent is actually a poor proxy for monopoly power, since most patents confer too little monopoly power to be a proper object of antitrust concern. Some patents confer no monopoly power at all. A patent may simply enable a firm to reduce the cost advantage of a competing firm; in such a case the patent might actually reduce the amount of monopoly power in the market."[5]

Further, legally protected products or processes, to the extent that they are commercially viable at all[6], generally are in competition with a variety of substitutes. For example, in one survey of licensors, the licensor faced no alternative supplier in only 27 per cent of the cases studied (see Table 2 below).

Table 2.   **Degree of supplier competition**[7]

Number of alternate supplier firms	Percentage
No other	27
2 to 5	34
5 to 10	10
10 to 15	9
15 to 20	10
Over 20	10

The study further found, as one might expect, that the returns to licensors decreased as the number of alternative suppliers increased[8]. Significant market power from a patent grant is seen as the exception rather than the rule[9], that market power is further restrained by the risk that reaping high returns will simply add to competitors incentives to seek to "invent around" the patent, limiting its value.

Recognizing that a patent or copyright may have little force economically is important if competition policy is to focus on those licensing practices which do pose a risk to competition. Merely presuming as, for example, the United States courts have done, that a patent or copyright creates market power risks the development of one-sided competition rules which fail to consider the possibility that a practice may not necessarily harm competition and indeed may be procompetitive. Further, the prohibition of such practices may unduly limit the returns to the creators of intellectual property out of exaggerated fears of anticompetitive impact.

2. *The leveraging of market power*

Even where an innovation creates market power, and substantial innovations should do just that, that market power has real limits in the demand curve for the new process or product. The innovator can justifiably seek to appropriate the consumer surplus created by the innovation, that is the reward function of the patent system, but can he gain more and "extend" or "leverage" his market power beyond that amount? That is, can he use a given amount of market power to gain additional market power, whether in the market for the original good or in a second market? A number of commentators have found the leverage hypothesis unconvincing[10].

Before discussing the hypothesis, however, it would useful to distinguish the concept of leveraging from the possible displacement of one firm by another with market power. For example, through a tie-in a firm with market power in the market for the tying good may acquire a substantial position in the market for the tied good, forcing the exit of some existing suppliers of the tied good. While this harms the firms thus forced to exit (and competition policy may for a variety of reasons be concerned over practices which force firms out in such a manner), the analysis which follows attempts to distinguish between harm to the firms forced out and harm to competition[11]. That is, the focus below is in seeking to determine whether licensing practices can help a firm reduce competition by increasing its market power, its power to price supracompetitively. The focus below is further restricted in that it does not take up the possibility that a firm will seek to use profits gained through its intellectual property rights to cross-subsidize efforts to drive out competitors from another market. This latter issue poses the question of predatory practices, which is the focus of a separate report recently prepared by the Committee on Competition Law and Policy[12].

Simple examples can show why leveraging is unconvincing. Suppose an innovator creates a new process which can lower the cost of a final product by ten per cent over the cost using existing technology. Manufacturers will be willing to pay for the use of the process, but not by more than the savings it generates, otherwise the old technology is the most cost-effective. If the innovator seeks to charge more he will simply price his innovation out of the market[13]. This assumes that the innovator has the only cost-saving process and thus a degree of market power. If there are other new cost-saving technologies available, the innovator's ability to raise the price is further constrained. Suppose the innovator resorts to tactics such as tie-ins, for example, tying the use of his process to a second, competitively sold input. Can he then leverage his market power? While tie-ins and similar tactics may, as discussed in the next section, help the innovator capture more of the surplus generated by his product, they would not, generally, help him to exceed it. Thus, the innovator could not sell a package of his process and a tied commodity for a price which would exceed the manufacturing cost of using

17

a less efficient process and purchasing the commodity on the open market[14]. On the other hand, as discussed in later paragraphs of this section, a tie-in may in certain circumstances permit a firm to gain a dominant market position.

Similar reasoning has been applied to product tie-ins. The innovator of a new consumer product faces a demand curve for that product which reflects the reservation price of each consumer. That demand curve again fixes for the innovator the maximum amount of consumer surplus he can seek to appropriate; raising prices will merely reduce consumption as consumers defect to substitute products. For example, each consumer may be willing to pay a premium to have the advantages of instant photography but only up to a point, beyond which he will turn to alternative technologies. The patentee may try to capture as much as possible of each consumer's premium through judicious pricing of the complementary goods which comprise the package, here cameras and proprietary film, but "tying" again does not increase the total amount of consumer surplus, just the proportion which can be captured[15].

By the same token, the bundling of intellectual property licences would not permit a licensor to exceed the surplus appropriable from a single item desired by a potential licensee. Suppose as before that a firm wanted to obtain a technology which could reduce its manufacturing costs by ten per cent, but could only obtain that license in conjunction with a license for another technology for which it had no use. Presumably it would be willing to accept the package, but not for a package price exceeding the costs saved, for otherwise less efficient technology would be more cost-effective[16].

Tie-ins and other surplus-capturing techniques may pose problems but they are specific. These problems are developed in Part C below. Note that the above analysis assumes that permitting innovators to fully appropriate their surpluses is pro-competitive. To the extent that the assumptions of competition policy in a given Member country are different from those stated herein, different policy conclusions on the appropriate treatment of intellectual property licensing agreements would likely follow.

B. BENEFITS TO COMPETITION THROUGH LICENSING

Commentators have argued that holders of intellectual property rights may use licensing agreements in attempting to accomplish a variety of goals which are not necessarily anticompetitive and indeed are probably procompetitive. For example, the terms of licensing agreements may operate to permit the licensor to increase the sales of his innovation, to permit him more easily to come to terms with licensees or to increase product quality or a licensee's productive efficiency. The activities just described also correspond to efforts by the licensor to increase the profitability of his exploitation of his intellectual property rights.

An important point of departure in analyzing these profit-enhancing aspects of licensing agreements is that those terms which can help an innovator capture the consumer surplus generated by his innovation is not anticompetitive; as suggested above, it may be seen as a gain to competition[17]. Further, to the extent that broader dissemination of improved technology is achieved through profit maximization, productive efficiency and thus consumer welfare are enhanced[18]. Finally, fulfilling the reward function of the intellectual property system serves to promote innovation and thus competition in the long run.

This point of departure includes several assumptions which may not be equally applicable in all Member countries. The first, discussed in the preceding section, is that competition policy is concerned with the preservation of competition rather than of particular competitors. From this point of view competition policy is neutral about practices which may displace one firm by another but which do not augment the second firm's market power. The second assumption is that competition policy seeks to maximize consumer welfare, an assumption which is complicated in some countries by competition laws which bring other factors to bear as well. There is an ongoing debate in Member countries concerning the extent to which competition policy should take account of political or social concerns beyond pure economic efficiency[19]. This Report does not take sides in such debates but raises the assumptions in an effort to clarify the bases of the analysis which follows. To the extent that the assumptions of competition policy in a given Member country are different from those stated herein, different policy conclusions on the appropriate treatment of intellectual property licensing agreements would likely follow.

Set forth below is a summary of points made by commentators who have attempted to identify those licensing activities which need not harm competition and indeed might be procompetitive. These points have been grouped into five broad categories of strategies: (1) to maximize profits[20], (2) to develop intellectual property and to enhance demand, (3) to manage risk and reduce transaction costs, (4) to maintain goodwill and (5) to promote productive efficiency. In examining the points set forth below it should be kept in mind that practically each practice which can be used procompetitively can also be used in other ways with clear anticompetitive effects. Those risks to competition are set forth in Section C below.

1. *Maximizing profits*

The intellectual property holder can engage in a variety of actions through licensing to try to gain the maximum profits possible out of his innovation. A number of these involve in one manner or another separating customers according to the value they place on the innovation and charging accordingly. If the licensor can thus capture the full consumer surplus of each consumer, i.e., perform perfect price discrimination, output is undoubtedly enhanced, because by doing so he has expanded output to the same extent that would occur in a perfectly competitive industry[21]. That is, he would expand output to the point where marginal revenue equalled marginal cost. If, however, the licensor cannot perfectly discriminate among consumers the results are less clear; output could either expand or contract over a monopolist's single-price output[22]. Some commentators have found that there is no way to determine a priori whether an imperfectly discriminating monopolist will expand or contract output because that effect depends upon the elasticities of demand of the various groups of consumers[23]. Others, however, have argued that output seems more likely to expand than to contract[24].

How competition officials view the output enhancing potential of price-discrimination can determine the outcome of particular cases. If one rejects the notion that such discrimination can increase output, one is less likely to find the discrimination desirable. On the other hand, some competition officials have explicitly found that price discrimination by a patent holder with market power generated a more competitive outcome than would have resulted under a non-discriminatory pricing structure[25].

Licensors may seek to price-discriminate in a variety of ways in licensing agreements. One way is through the use of a tie-in to "meter" the intensity with which a protected machine or process is used and to adjust the amounts paid according to the intensity of use[26]. This can be done by charging less than the single monopoly price for the protected product or process

19

and a higher-than-market price for a tied commodity used in the manufacturing process. Tying could be procompetitive here because it results in greater diffusion of the product or process than would occur if the licensor charged a single monopoly price and did not tie, as the tie-in makes diffusion to light users possible[27].

Similar reasoning can be applied to other efforts to price the protected item according to the elasticity of demand of different consumers or groups of consumers. Thus pricing according to different fields of use can both increase returns to the licensor and bring use of the innovation within reach of consumers who would be unwilling or unable to pay the single monopoly price in their field of use. Similar differences across geographic markets can again bring both higher output and greater returns through price discrimination[28].

A necessary condition for the licensor to be able to price according to consumers' elasticity of demand is that he be able to block arbitrage by consumers receiving lower prices[29]. Thus, effective price discrimination may require territorial or field-of-use restrictions, including restrictions against resale to consumers in other geographic or product markets. Efforts to price-discriminate across different groups of consumers also may involve, where the licensee resells the patented product or an unpatented product manufactured with a patented process, the use of price restraints. For example, although resale price maintenance is objectionable in a variety of contexts, e.g. where used to facilitate collusion at either the manufacturer or dealer level, those concerns may be absent if it is shown that the sole purpose is to ensure that the effort to price-discriminate is effective at the level of the final consumer.

2. *Intellectual Property Development and Demand Enhancement*

The owner of intellectual property may use restrictions to increase the incentives for a licensee to develop the innovation by protecting the licensee from the "free-riding" on those developments by other licensees. For example, so called "field-of-use" restrictions can guarantee a licensee who develops improvements which are not patentable in a particular field of use that other licensees (or even the licensor) who contributed nothing to the improvement will not be able to appropriate its economic benefits.

A manufacturer of a protected product may also seek through restrictions in distribution agreements to shift outward the demand curve for his product, particularly if the product is complex and requires some presale promotion to stimulate consumer demand[30]. Thus the licensor may seek to create incentives for his distributors to invest in advertising and showroom demonstrations. Incentives to provide post-sale service can also be important again particularly where the product is complex[31]. Here the licensor is primarily concerned with avoiding free rider problems which can reduce a dealer's incentives to perform as desired[32].

These procompetitive effects of what are essentially vertical arrangements should be considered in light of possible anticompetitive effects from the same practices. For example, tie-ins may help a firm raise barriers to entry or to gain a dominant position in the second market, as discussed in the previous section. Territorial, customer or field-of-use restrictions may be part of a cartel agreement to divide markets, as discussed in Part C below. Likewise, pricing restrictions, also discussed below, may be part of a cartel agreement at either the licensor or licensee level.

20

3. *Managing Risk and Transaction Costs*

There are a variety of ways that a licensor can use licensing restrictions to reduce the level of risk facing him or his potential licensees, including risks stemming from uncertainty about the utility of the licensed product or process, uncertainty about demand for the licensed product or for a product made using a licensed process, uncertainty about the outcome of litigation and uncertainty about the abilities of the licensee. As will be developed more fully below, a number of these uncertainties can be viewed as simply a reflection of the high cost of gaining additional information, especially about the value of the licence and the abilities and desires of the licensee. To the extent that risk facing one or both parties to a licence can be reduced, expected returns are increased and an increased diffusion of the licensed item should result.

A number of the risks just described can be reduced by tie-ins as described in the preceding section. For example, a metering tie-in can be used to permit the creation of more attractive package to the potential licensee unsure of the value of a new machine[33]. The purchase or lease price of the machine is reduced and the licensor's profits are gained according to intensity of the licensee's use as measured by the tie-in. Thus an uncertain licensee is able to test a new machine or process with less at risk than if he had to pay a single monopoly price with no tie-in. The licensor gains his return only to the extent that his innovation actually benefits the licensee.

Similarly, a tie-in can be used to manage the risk to the licensor that the licensee will be unsuccessful[34]. When a licensor is faced with numerous possible licensees, especially new firms in rapidly growing fields, he is faced with the risk that the firm(s) he licenses will fail and, conversely, that a firm using competing technology will succeed and grow. Because identifying the likely winners in advance is costly and probably impossible, the licensor can seek to reduce his risk by placing the innovation with as many firms as possible. A tie-in can help the innovator to price his product or process low and to gain his rents from the eventual heavy use by the successful firms. By the same token, a tie-in can reduce risk to the licensee uncertain of its own future or of the consumer demand for the particular product[35].

Pure know-how licences pose particular risks which can be reduced by tie-ins or royalty terms. It can be difficult for a potential licensee to agree in advance to pay for know-how when he does not yet know what that information is or how well it will work in practice. The innovator will, however, be reluctant to share his confidential information without a binding agreement. A metering tie-in agreement can bridge that gap[36]. A similar result can be obtained by an agreement which assesses royalties on output utilizing the technology.

A patentee faces the risk that once it licenses its new product or process, the licensee will have insights leading to improvements patents once it gains experience with the innovation. Thus the licensor risks either being surpassed or blocked by the licensees it does business with[37]. Grantback clauses which permit the licensor to use the improvement thus can avoid this risk. Exclusive grantbacks have been said to give patent holders excessive control over the product and may serve to extend the time period of protection beyond that contained in the original patent grant[38], thus non-exclusive grantback clauses have been said to pose fewer risks to competition. That view is not unanimous, however, as others argue that exclusive grantbacks can be procompetitive[39].

Related to grantback clauses are commitments by licensors to provide licensees with access to improvements in the licensed technology. Such a committment is procompetitive in that it reduces risk to the licensee that its technology will be soon made obsolete. By reducing that risk, an improvements clause increases both the likelihood of licensing and the investment the licensee will be willing to make in the acquired technology[40].

A patentee may be confronted with conflicting claims of other patentees, producing claims of mutual infringement. These conflicts are costly to resolve through litigation and pose obvious risks to the patentees. Patent pooling agreements can be used to settle such disagreements without resort to litigation[41]. Such pooling agreements can be procompetitive in that by reducing the risk of litigation, they increase the expected return to the innovator and thus make innovation a more attractive activity economically. Patent pools can also be useful in resolving conflicts arising out of blocking patents, permitting competing patentees to each use the combined technology[42].

Pooling agreements can also be used purely as methods to reduce the transaction costs involved in the negotiation of individual licenses. While this can occur with patent pools[43], it can also arise with pools of copyrighted material. In the latter situation the transaction costs of individually negotiated licences could be prohibitive in light of the royalties involved, making a pooling arrangement the only economic method to license to myriad users.

Another risk facing a licensor with multiple products to license is that because he cannot, except perhaps through costly bargaining, know the value each potential licensee places on each separate licence, he will not price in an optimal fashion. This risk can be overcome and transaction costs saved by grouping licences into packages and offering them for a flat fee[44]. This practice has a procompetitive effect in increasing the diffusion of innovations by saving transaction costs. Further, by reducing the licensor's costs, a given expected return on innovation can be achieved at a lower per licence price.

4. *Maintaining a reputation for quality*

A licensor may seek to use restrictions in a licensing agreement in a variety of ways to maintain his reputation for quality. One is to tie the use of a protected product or process to the purchase of some other input affecting the product's operation or the efficiency of the process[45]. This could be important in complex products or processes where unsatisfactory operation cannot readily be traced to an inferior quality input, permitting other suppliers of that input to reduce quality at the expense of the licensor's reputation, a type of free-rider problem[46]. Licensors may wish to take over this quality control function by either manufacturing or purchasing the input and supplying it to licensees. Presumably this will be done whenever the cost of doing so is less than the cost of specifying the quality of the input and ensuring that independent suppliers meet that specification[47].

Another type of quality control function is related to the quality of pre- and post-sale services provided by dealers in patented products, a point essentially similar to that covered in section 2 above.

5. *Maintaining productive efficiency by the licensee*

A patentee may face a particular problem when his patent is on a product which is used as an input in manufacturing another product and is not required to be used in a fixed proportion in the manufacturing process. That is, the same quantity of final output can be obtained by using various proportions of the patented input and other inputs. The problem essentially is that the patentee's consumers will select the proportion of patented/non-patented inputs according to the relative prices of those inputs. To the extent that the patentee seeks to capture the surplus generated by his input, he induces his licensees to substitute other, less efficient inputs for his, reducing their productive efficiency and possibly limiting the overall market for the final product[48].

Bowman has argued that the patentee can seek to overcome this problem in several ways. One way would be to tie the purchase of his input with the others and supply them all in optimal proportions, taking his surplus on the bundle of inputs[49]. Another would be to charge his royalty on sales of the final product rather than on the patented input, leaving the licensee with an incentive to manufacture in the most efficient manner possible[50].

The above sections provide a general sense of the procompetitive rationales which have been presented for many restrictions in patent licensing agreements. Notably, nearly all of these procompetitive results are found when the relationship between the licensor and licensee is vertical; the protected product or process is being used as an input by a downstream licensee or the licensee is serving as a distributor of the licensor's product. By contrast, the concerns over anticompetitive consequences, as the next section will show, by and large relate to the possible elimination of actual or potential competition between horizontal competitors. When studying the pro- and anticompetitive effects of the licence of an intellectual property right, it should be carefully analyzed whether the licensee is a potential competitor, even if the relationship of the two, on appearance, is vertical.

C.   RISKS TO COMPETITION

The previous discussion has presented arguments that certain aspects of licensing agreements, particularly those which operate in a vertical fashion, need not harm competition and may be procompetitive in their impact. Arguments have also been suggested that some presumptions relating to the market power created by the grant of intellectual property rights and the impact of tie-ins may not be properly grounded in economics. All this is not to say, however, that competition policy is not properly concerned about licensing agreements. In fact, serious anticompetitive effects can arise, especially when the licensor and licensee are actual or potential competitors. This section identifies those areas of greatest concern.

1.   *Cartelization*

The single greatest concern facing competition authorities when reviewing intellectual property licensing agreements is that the agreement is a vehicle for a cartel arrangement to fix prices, limit output or divide markets. Although this concern can be briefly stated, it is the most serious threat to competition found in such licensing agreements. It can arise whenever the agreement is between actual or potential competitors in a given market. Notably, those competitors can be either the licensors or the licensees and the market to be cartelized need not be the market which is the subject of the licensing agreement[51]. Further, the elimination of competition can occur in any of several markets: the market for products manufactured using the technology or in the market for the technology itself. Thus, a patent pooling or cross-licensing agreement between competing licensors can reduce competition in the market for those technologies or in downstream product markets using the technology as an input where the agreement includes restrictions relating to prices, territories, customers, fields of use or "output"[52].

Some commentators have argued that insight into whether a licensing agreement is a vehicle for a cartel arrangement can be gained by assessing the strength of the technology being licensed[53]. Under this view an agreement which is horizontal in nature is especially suspect when there is a weak patent involved or the technology is not of great importance to the licensee. The problem with this approach is that it is often difficult to assess either the strength of the patent or its commercial significance. Thus a better initial question is whether the agreement is a sham, i.e. where the parties demonstrably are not interested in transferring intellectual property rights, but rather are using the licence to disguise their effort to restrict output or raise prices in some market other than the market for the intellectual property[54]. That assessment is more difficult, however, when the agreement involves predominantly know-how, as there is greater uncertainty over the composition of the knowledge being transferred[55].

Assuming that the agreement is not a sham, competition authorities need to determine the potential for cartelization to stem from it. An important method to test the likelihood of cartelization from a licensing agreement between actual or potential competitors is to consider how much of the relevant market is subject to the restrictions. A licensing restriction between firms controlling a substantial market share obviously poses greater risk of effective cartelization than an agreement between two fringe firms.

The previous paragraphs identified problems where the cartel agreement is embodied in the licensing agreement. In addition, licensing agreements may serve to facilitate the implementation of separate cartel understandings. For example, cartelization is facilitated to the extent that the product is homogeneous rather than differentiated[56]. Thus licensing agreements which specify the design or technology to be used in producing a product may serve to facilitate a separate collusive arrangement between the licensor and licensee to fix the price of that product. This problem may especially arise in patent pooling agreements[57].

Similarly, cartel agreements by *licensees* can be implemented by ostensibly vertical distribution agreements. For example, this could occur if they induced their licensors to impose resale price maintenance, thus fixing prices at the licensee level[58]. However, to be effective in reducing competition such restraints would have to apply to a substantial proportion of firms at the licensee level, otherwise the cartelizing licensees would be vulnerable to competition from non-restrained firms[59].

Vertical price fixing may also contribute to the stability of a cartel arrangement at the licensor level by making the licensors' retail prices more transparent and stable[60]. Thus a price-fixing arrangement among competing licensors in which each licensor engages in resale price maintenance with its distributors is more likely to be stable than one which does not involve resale price maintenance by making non-compliance with the cartel more obvious and thus less likely to occur. Another source of instability is removed by preventing independant price cutting by distributors and by enlisting them in the surveillance of local prices. Other vertical restraints such as restraints on output, territories or customers may also facilitate collusion at the licensor level to the extent that they are widely and uniformly utilized[61].

Finally, it has been suggested that tie-in agreements may facilitate horizontal collusion among licensors if the licensors use them as a device to detect cheating on a cartel agreement. In the previous section it was described how a metering tie-in could be used in a procompetitive fashion by a firm seeking to charge according to the intensity of use. In those examples the tied good was assumed to be priced above the market price in order to compensate for below-market pricing of the tying good and capture the consumer surplus. One commentator, however, has argued that if there is a price fixing arrangement governing the price of the tied good, then what appears to be a metering-type tie-in arrangement may really have an additional function, to detect non-compliance with the cartel arrangement. This can happen if the licensor offers to match any price on the tied good reported to him by the licensee. Thus, oddly enough, an offer to sell the tied good at the "market" price rather than supra competitively may operate to reduce competition[62].

2. *Exclusionary effects*

Competition authorities are also properly concerned that a licence agreement not operate to exclude anticompetitively other firms. That is, that the licence's features not serve to create market power or facilitate collusive activities. This of course is different from the exclusionary effect found in any exclusive contract. This concern, previously mentioned with respect to tie-ins, is that the vertical restriction not operate to substantially raise barriers to entry by requiring entry at more than one level. In terms of tie-ins, the concern is that the licensor will gain a dominant position in the market for the tied good, thus forcing its potential competitors to enter both markets simultaneously. Whether gaining a large market share in the market for the tied good leads to increased market power depends upon the barriers to entry and expansion in that market[63].

There can be similar exclusionary problems if there is an exclusivity or "tie-out" arrangement with licensees, that is, that the licensees employ only the licensor's technology, freezing out other potential licensors. If such an arrangement involved so many licensees that entry at the licensor level required simultaneous entry at the licensee level *and* that entry was difficult, then there would be justifiable concern that the licensor had reduced or eliminated potential competition at the licensor level. This concern is similar to the concern raised above about a licensor gaining a dominant position in the market for a tied good; the possible anticompetitive effect depends upon the conditions of entry in the second market. To the extent that entry there is relatively easy, the licensor will not have gained market power even if he has acquired a large market share[64].

Another type of exclusionary effect relates to practices which impede the development of competing new technologies. This can come about through licences with exclusive grant-back provisions which operate to eliminate the licensees' incentives to develop alternative technology. This problem can arise either through the actions of a single licensor or through the terms of a patent pool. The creation of competing technology can also be impeded by exclusivity or "tie-out" provisions which, if they cover a large enough portion of potential licensees, effectively closes the market to other potential innovators[65].

The risks of anticompetitive effects from exclusionary conduct of the types referred to above thus depend heavily upon the structure of the relevant markets. Three conditions are necessary for anticompetitive effects vis-à-vis consumers. The first is that the market in which the firm or firms imposing the restraint operate (and which is supposed not to be performing competitively) be very highly concentrated, with the leading firms in that market using the same restraints or restraints having the same effect. Second, the restraints must cover most of the capacity in the market being foreclosed to competitors. Finally, entry into the foreclosed market must be difficult[66]. If any of these conditions are absent, the licensors will not be able to co-ordinate their activities in order to gain market power, shielded from the threat of new entry. For example, if entry is easy at the licensee level, efforts by a group of licensors to cartelize the licensor level using exclusive licensee arrangements to freeze out fringe licensors would fail, as any rents would attract entry by new potential licensees for the excluded licensors. If the licensors held only a modest share of the market at the licensee level, they would have even less success raising prices in that market. Finally, if the licensors were too numerous, their efforts to agree to and enforce a cartel agreement would be likely to fail.

3. *Acquiring market power*

Intellectual property rights can be used to acquire market power apart from the exclusionary practices discussed above. This market power can be created in the market for the technology itself or in a product market if the technology is a necessary input in the product. Such problems can arise when a licensor simply purchases exclusive rights in competing technology. Licensing agreements which convey such rights can be analysed in the same fashion as horizontal mergers, that is, by looking at the market shares controlled by the competing technologies. Market share figures can be misleading in technology transfers, however, as a new technology with a minuscule share could rapidly become the dominant technology in the future[67]. Also, the availability of market share data for a given technology market is not only limited but also harder to evaluate compared with market share data for a product market. Thus, some judgement needs to be exercised in analysing market share data.

4. *Non-price predation*

Copyrights, patents and trade secrets can be used as tools of non-price predation by a firm which brings legal proceedings in bad faith in order to exclude rivals[68]. While abusive enforcement is not, strictly speaking, a licensing practice, the anticompetitive potential is clear. Firms developing new technologies may not have the resources to engage in extended litigation with established firms and thus may be excluded entirely from competing. At the least, a firm's entry may be delayed and its costs raised disproportionately to those of its established rival.

Abusive litigation must be distinguished however from good faith enforcement of intellectual property rights. The value of intellectual property rights depends on the ability of the rights holder to prevent others from copying his innovation, thus access to courts or other enforcement bodies is necessary in any effective IPR regime. While a good faith litigant may of course lose in court, that situation is distinct from where the procedure is a sham aimed solely at imposing burdens on the rival.

Abusive litigation represents only the most egregious form of non-price predation. Non-price predation can be viewed more broadly to include any conduct designed to exclude rivals or to raise their costs on a basis other than efficiency. Thus, the conduct outlined in the two preceding sections and other restrictions would be seen by some writers and competition authorities as non-price predation, also known as conduct to raise rivals' costs. One problem facing competition authorities in this area is to distinguish between the various types of conduct which can raise rivals' costs and to attack only those which are not based on efficiency.

The preceding sections have identified the major arguments on the pro- and anticompetitive aspects of intellectual property licensing agreements, along with the policy assumptions upon which those arguments are based. Notably, it was seen that many clauses, looked at in isolation, are neither "good" nor "bad" from the point of view of competition policy; a particular type of clause such as a tie-in can be used for a variety of different purposes and have similarly varied effects on competition. This points up the importance of an inquiry into the purpose and likely effect of clauses in their economic context, including an examination of the horizontal or vertical relationship between licensor and licensee. Leaving apart sham agreements, this examination will likely involve a balancing of the risks of cartelization or other effects increasing market power against the benefits of the licensing arrangement.

Having identified these arguments, the next two chapters of the Report will turn to the situations in various Member countries to see to what extent these points have been accepted or rejected in national competition policy. Chapter IV will present the legislative framework in Member countries while Chapter V will review significant decisions by courts and competition policy enforcement officials in the area of intellectual property licensing.

Chapter 4

LEGAL MECHANISMS REGULATING PATENT
AND KNOW-HOW LICENSING

This chapter presents the competition laws and policies which apply to intellectual property licensing agreements in Member countries. These include both generally applicable competition laws, special statutory provisions related to intellectual property, currently applicable regulations, other forms of administrative guidance, and proposed legislation and regulations.

Some regulations will be described only in general terms at this point with the detailed discussion reserved for Chapter 5. Chapter 5 will discuss representative cases on patent and know-how licensing according to the major types of clauses found in licensing contracts. Where a regulation is organized in a clause-by-clause fashion, the details of that regulation will be presented in Chapter 5 rather than here.

This chapter generally excludes those laws and regulations which govern intellectual property rights other than patents or know-how. Thus, trademarks and issues related to franchising are not covered. Copyright-protected artistic expression is also excluded. On the other hand, policies concerning vertical practices unrelated to intellectual property will be cited where appropriate as the analysis of such arrangements is often directly applicable to the analysis of vertical licensing agreements.

Australia

Anticompetitive conduct in Australia is regulated through the provisions of the Trade Practices Act 1974. Sections 45 to 50A of that Act contain general prohibitions of a range of restrictive business practices, including both horizontal arrangements such as price agreements among competitors and vertical arrangements such as exclusive dealing or tied purchasing and resale price maintenance. Misuse of market power is also prohibited. Exemption from the application of the Act to some of these prohibited practices can be obtained through an administrative procedure of authorisation by the competition authority, the Trade Practices Commission. Authorisation can be granted by the Commission on public benefit grounds, notwithstanding that the conduct in question may otherwise contravene the competition provisions of the Act.

Apart from the availability of administrative procedures such as authorisation, the Act also provides automatic exemption from the application of its competition provisions in respect of certain activities already regulated through other laws or policies. This includes a specific exemption in relation to certain actions concerning patents, trade marks, designs or copyright. This is achieved through application of section 51 of the Act.

Section 51(1) provides a blanket exemption from the competition provisions for conduct specifically authorised by federal or state legislation other than laws relating to patents, trade marks, designs or copyright. For conduct relating to these forms of intellectual property, Section 51(2) provides a limited exemption from the Trade Practices Act. The prohibitions against misuse of market power (Section 46) and resale price maintenance (Section 48) however remain in force. The exemption of Section 51(3) applies only to patent license conditions which relate to the patented invention or to articles made by that invention.

The Industrial Property Advisory Committee's (IPAC) report *Patents, Competition and Innovation in Australia* examined the interaction of patent rights and competition law. IPAC recommended revising the exemption provided under Section 51(3) for patent related conduct by, inter alia, proscribing patent-related conduct which has the purpose, effect or likely effect of substantially lessening competition.

IPAC's recommendations in this area were not accepted by the government because the report had not provided evidence of any substantial problems in practice with the present provisions of the Trade Practices Act and the Patents Act and had not established a case for the policy change suggested. Furthermore, implementation of the recommendations would have introduced major inconsistencies in the way the Trade Practices Act was applied to patent-related conduct and other anticompetitive conduct in general. Similar inconsistencies would also have arisen in relation to conduct involving intellectual property rights other than patents.

The Copyright Law Review Committee is currently considering whether any changes should be made to the importation provisions of the Copyright Act. Those provisions make it an infringement of copyright for a person knowingly, without the permission of the copyright owner, to import or distribute copyright materials for various commercial purposes. The Committee is also considering whether streamlining amendments should be made to section 135 of the Copyright Act, which provides for customs seizure of printed works, the importation of which is objected to by the copyright owners, and whether section 135 should be extended to, in effect, computer software, films and sound recordings. The Committee is in the final stages of its review.

Consideration of the competition aspects of new forms of property rights arose during consideration of the Plant Variety Rights Act enacted in March 1987. The Act allows plant breeders to apply for a grant of proprietary rights over any new variety of plants which they may develop. The objective is to encourage the development of new plant varieties by enabling plant breeders, through the grant of exclusive rights to produce and sell varieties they develop, to recoup some of the high research and development costs involved.

In many respects, the plant variety rights under this legislation are similar to existing intellectual property rights and thus raise similar issues from a competition policy perspective. Granting plant variety rights should promote competition in the industry by making plant breeding more commercially attractive. However, any anticompetitive conduct will be subject to the Trade Practices Act, with the exception of conduct relating to the exclusive rights specifically authorised by the Plant Variety Rights Act. Note that the Plant Variety Rights Act requires the grantee to make the plant variety publicly available in reasonable quantities and at reasonable prices.

It is anticipated that issues of this kind will continue to arise as technological development leads to the creation of new forms of property not protected by existing intellectual property legislation and, as a consequence, remedial legislation is put forward to ensure that developers' rights are protected.

Austria

In Austria, the 1972 Cartels Act provided that restraints of competition in connection with the licensing of industrial property rights which do not exceed the scope of the protected right are not subject to the Act based upon the "theory on the scope of protected rights" (Schutzrechtstheorie). Section 22 of the Patents Act defines the protected rights. The patent vests exclusive authority in the patentee to produce the subject of the invention industrially, to put it on the market, to offer it for sale and to work it. Thus, restrictions on the licensee in respect of type, extent, quantity, territory and time are in principle not subject to cartel law. This policy of protected rights continues unchanged under the new Cartels Act adopted in 1988, Federal Law Gazette 600/1988.

In addition, the Cartels Act is interpreted restrictively under Austrian case law as a regulation limiting the freedom of contract. Anticompetitive agreements contained in a contract which primarily serves other purposes are thus not considered to constitute a cartel. Restrictions of competition in connection with licensing agreements may, however, establish a cartel if they are in the common interest of both contracting parties. Such a common interest may be served, for example, in the case of collective licences and several partners, as in the case, for instance, of exclusive territories.

The Austrian Patents Act contains provisions against the abuse of patent rights. If a contract stipulates that a person who acquires a patent right has to refrain from a specific gainful activity or, in the exercise of such gainful activity, has to comply with certain restrictions which do not relate solely to the manner or extent of working the patented invention, the Federal Minister of Economic Affairs may declare such stipulation to be wholly or partly invalid if public interests are thereby prejudiced (Section 38 of the Patents Act). This possibility applies in particular (Section 39 of the Patents Act) to agreements prohibiting the licensee from manufacturing, putting on the market, offering for sale or using products for the manufacture of which the patented invention is not needed or for employing a process not covered by the patent. No decisions hve been taken on the basis of these two sections of the Patents Act in recent years.

If a licence agreement requires a licensee to obtain materials, machinery or substances needed for the manufacture of a licensed article from the licensor or a third person designated by him for the sole purpose of ensuring constant quality, such a requirement is not considered to be anticompetitive. On the other hand, if a licensing agreement contains the mutual obligation of the patent owners to refrain from price competition, it is a cartel agreement.

Finally, Section 36 of the Patents Act contains provisions governing compulsory licenses. These provisions apply, for example, to blocking patents where a patented invention is not worked sufficiently in Austria and where the public interest requires that a licence be granted.

Belgium

Patent licensing practices in Belgium are subject to the Patent Law of 28th March 1984 as well as to the Act of 27th May 1960 Against the Abuse of Economic Power. This patent law, while generally not directed towards the issues of this report, does contain several relevant provisions. In particular, Article 28, 2) codifies the doctrine of exhaustion of rights, stating that patent rights do not extend to products once they have been introduced into Belgium by the patentee or with his express consent. Article 31 provides that compulsory licences may be granted for dormant or insufficiently exploited patents in Belgium or in the case of a blocking patent. Under Article 44, all patent assignments must be registered to be enforceable against third parties.

Patent licences can be exclusive or non-exclusive and for all or part of Belgium but must be in writing and notified to the Industrial Property Office of the Ministry of Economic Affairs[1]. Licence tranfers must also be in writing and notified to the Industrial Property Office[2]. Licensing contracts remain valid even though a patent is later ruled invalid, absent bad faith by or unjust enrichment of the patentee, but the licensee can seek some restitution, to the extent justified by the circumstances, of sums paid under the contract[3]. Finally, exclusive jurisdiction lies with the "tribunaux de première instance" for all actions involving infringement or unfair competition related to infringement.

Notably, the patent law does not exclude the operation of the 1960 Act against patent licensing practices which abuse a dominant position. The legislative history of the 1960 Act indicates that a number of patent licensing practices could be found to be an abuse[4]. In particular, the legislators state that an abuse under Article 2 of that law can exist due to practices which tend to elevate prices, price discriminate, limit quantities or share markets. Exclusive dealing can be an abuse if the goal is to exclude competitors. Also considered to be abusive are all practices aimed at restricting the use of a patent which could increase product quality, reduce price or produce better or cheaper substitute products in the absence of a justification on public interest grounds. The Senate also cited specifically the acquisition of patents by a competitor to prevent the emergence of a competitive technology[5].

Canada

Four sections of Canada's Competition Act (R.S., c. C-23, as amended) refer specifically to intellectual property rights: Section 29 dealing with abuse of patents and trade marks, Section 38 relating to price maintenance, Section 51 concerning abuse of dominant position, and Section 57 relating to specialisation agreements.

Section 29 of the Act provides remedies to deal with situations in which patents, trade marks or copyrights are used to restrain trade or commerce. Under this section the Attorney General may apply to the Federal Court of Canada for an order nullifying a licensing agreement or enjoining its exercise. In addition, the order may provide for compulsory licences or even revoke the patent. These remedies can be triggered when a patent has been used to "unduly" limit production of an article or commodity or to unreasonably restrain trade, enhance price or reduce competition. This section relates to "articles or commodities"; restraints affecting services are not covered. On the other hand, it does not appear that the commodity or article affected need be the one benefiting from the patent; tie-in practices, for example, seem to be within the reach of Section 29.

Section 29 does include a rule of reason test in its requirement of undue or unreasonable effects. This is the same test that is found in the section of the Act dealing with conspiracies in restraint of trade. The cases brought under that section suggest that the test of undueness embodies a high threshold of anti-competitive effects. In fact, applications under Section 29 have been made by the Attorney General in only two cases during the past three decades.

Another section of the Competition Act that applies specifically to intellectual property rights is Section 38 dealing with price maintenance. That section prohibits, inter alia, holders of exclusive patent rights from seeking to maintain resale prices by, e.g., agreements, coercion or refusal to supply a discounter. Violations of Section 38 are a criminal offence subject to fines and up to five years of imprisonment, but several exemptions are set out in subsection 38(9). For example, paragraph 38(9)(d) provides an exception from subsection 38(1)(b) (refusal to supply) in situations where a distributor fails to provide a level of service that may be reasonably expected by consumers. Another exception is provided in situations where a product is being used for loss leading.

A third provision of the Competition Act which refers specifically to intellectual property rights is Section 51 dealing with abuse of dominant position. Section 51 is a non-criminal provision which provides remedies for a broad range of potentially anti-competitive acts. An illustrative list of such acts is provided in Section 50 of the legislation. The list indicates that the anti-competitive acts that may be dealt with under Section 51 include acts such as: *(i)* pre-emption of scarce facilities or resources required by a competitor for the operation of a business, with the object of withholding the facilities or resources from a market, *(ii)* adoption of product specifications that are incompatible with products produced by any other person and are designed to prevent his entry into or to eliminate him from a market; or *(iii)* requiring or inducing a supplier to sell only or primarily to certain customers or to refrain from selling to a competitor with the object of preventing a competitor's entry into or expansion in a market.

Subsection 51(5) indicates that Section 51 is not intended to affect the legitimate exercise of intellectual or industrial property rights. The wording covers not only express rights but also interests derived under the intellectual property statutes. Subsection 51(5) does not, however, provide a blanket exemption for intellectual property rights holders from the application of the section. The use of the phrase "pursuant only to the exercise of any right ..." suggests that Section 51 remains applicable to the use of such rights in ways which go beyond the purposes contemplated in the statutes.

Even in situations where Section 51 may apply to the use of intellectual property rights, the application of the section requires an in-depth evaluation of the competitive effects of specific acts. Subsection 51(1) requires proof of three specific elements: *(i)* that the firm(s) involved substantially or completely control a class or species of business; *(ii)* that the firm(s) have engaged in a practice (as distinct from an isolated instance) of anti-competitive acts; and *(iii)* that the practice of anti-competitive acts has had the effect of lessening competition substantially. In addition, subsection 51(4) of the Act requires the Competition Tribunal to consider whether a practice is the result of superior competitive performance.

In most cases the remedy available under Section 51 is likely to be limited to an order prohibiting the specific anti-competitive acts. Subsection 51(2) indicates that, in cases where a mere prohibition order is unlikely be sufficient, the Tribunal may make such other orders as are necessary to overcome the effects of the anti-competitive acts. However, in view of subsection 51(3), which provides that orders made under subsection 51(2) should interfere with the rights of any persons affected only to the extent that is necessary, the scope of such orders is likely to be limited.

Section 58 of the Competition Act provides a civil review process to deal with specialization agreements, which may involve aspects of cross-licensing or patent pooling. Subsection 58(4) authorizes the Competition Tribunal to make orders respecting the wider licensing of patents as a condition for registration of a specialization agreement.

The purpose of these provisions relating to specialisation agreements is to permit the operation of such agreements, notwithstanding the potential application of relevant provisions of the Act, where the agreements are considered to be desirable for efficiency reasons. The provision for orders, respecting the wider licensing of patents, along with the other orders available under subsection 58(4), provides a means of counterbalancing the potential anti-competitive impact of such agreements.

In addition to the above-noted provisions that refer specifically to intellectual property rights, the exercise of such rights could also be affected by other, more general sections of the Act relating to restraints to competition. These could include Section 32 dealing with conspiracies in restraint of trade, Section 47 relating to refusal to deal and Section 49 concerning tied selling, exclusive dealing and market restriction. Finally, it should be noted that certain provisions (Sections 67-73) of the Patent Act also provide remedies to deal with abusive conduct, principally in the sense of failure to work a patent on commercial scale in Canada. The application of these sections is discussed in the forthcoming study *Competition Policy Treatment of Intellectual Property Licensing*.

Denmark

Patent licensing practices in Denmark are subject to both the Danish competition-related statutes, the Monopolies and Restrictive Practices Supervision Act of 1955 and The Prices and Profits Act of 1974, as well as to the Patents Act of 1967. The Monopolies Act is based on a principle of abuse. Only resale price maintenance is specifically prohibited. Agreements which exert substantial influence on market conditions must be notified to the Monopolies Control Authority (MCA), which can apply the Monopolies Act to firms which have a substantial influence on market conditions[6] and which may cause unreasonable prices or terms of business[7]. The reasonableness of prices follows from an examination of business conditions based on the conditions of firms which are operated with appropriate technical and commercial efficiency[8]. Enforcement tools include the issuance of orders to cease violations, including orders to supply and orders which specify permissible prices[9].

The Monopolies Act and the Patents Act are based on conflicting considerations given that the aim of the Monopolies Act is to promote freedom of trade, freedom which is restricted through the Patents Act and other rules protecting intangible rights to promote creative works.

According to Section 45 of the Patents Act, the Maritime and Commercial Court may grant a compulsory licence in case of non-use. There is no case law under the 1967 Patents Act, but in 1966 the Court granted a compulsory licence concerning a preparation from the pharmaceutical industry, which is normally rather reluctant to grant voluntary licences and as such makes the compulsory licence rules useful. Earlier practice also shows examples of compulsory licences in case of non-use, i.a. concerning pharmaceutical products and incandescent lamps.

According to Section 47 of the Patents Act, the Maritime and Commercial Court can also grant a compulsory licence when required by important general interests, as for instance State security, supply of medicines and food, energy supply, communication services etc. According to legal theory[10], it is doubtful whether - or to what extent - the rules are applicable to the pricing of patented services.

The preamble to Section 47 states that "if the patent appears to be utilized in a subversive way, the existing legislation on monopolies gives a much better chance than previously of controlling price problems, and the rules on compulsory licencing make it possible to create competition"[11]. In practice, however, the MCA has never taken measures against the pricing of individual patented products, and as a result of Section 12, Subsection 5, of the Monopolies Act, according to which the general principle of assessment on the basis of cost allocation on the individual products may be disregarded, the MCA has no possibility - except on very rare occasions - to intervene against the pricing of individual patented products.

Concerning the patent right as such, subsequent measures can be taken according to the Monopolies Act against unreasonable anti-competitive practices. In the competition law literature, the fundamental point of view is that only normal utilisation of individual or collective rights escapes intervention under the Monopolies Act. Thus, for collective rights, "as soon as it concerns major groups of incorporeal rights which are to be utilized by organizations, associations etc., one is beyond the typical normal utilization as provided in the legislation on exclusive rights"[12].

No Danish court decision has yet clarified the conflicting considerations of the Monopolies Act and the Patents Act. The MCA's administration of the Monopolies Act, however, is similar to that suggested by legal theory. In a report on the pharmaceutical sector in Denmark the MCA states that "the utilization of restrictive practices based on patent rights falls under the legislation on prices and monopolies and is subject to control in pursuance of this legislation. It is evident, however, that interventions against unreasonable effects of the practising of a patent right are subject to deference to social considerations which justify the legal exclusive right obtained by the patent ..."[13].

Except for the case mentioned below in chapter 5 Section D, there is no Danish case law concerning the application of competition legislation to intellectual property rights such as patent licence agreements and know-how licence agreements.

France

The relationship between French competition and intellectual property laws is not defined by statute. Rights under French patent law, which in any event are exhausted once a patented item is put into commerce by the patentee or with his consent, do not constitute an exemption from the operation of competition law. Further, the application of French competition law to practices involving intellectual property rights was expressly established by the Competition Commission's 1955 *Magnesium Industry* decision, discussed in detail in the next chapter. Thus, French competition law is fully applicable to patent and know-how licensing practices. Under the competition law, a licence term is illegal, and legally void, if it amounts to an anticompetitive practice, i.e. if it involves cartel conduct, an abuse of dominant position or an abuse of economic dependency. These prohibitions are set forth in the competition policy provisions beginning with Article 50 of the Ordonnance of 30th June 1945, recently recodified by Articles 7, 8 and 9 of the Competition Ordonnance of 1986.

Article 50 prohibited all agreements having the object or possible effect of restraining or distorting competition. Singled out specifically were practices restricting resale prices, encouraging artificial price changes, hindering technical advance or hindering the freedom of other firms to compete. Prohibited agreements are void as a matter of law. Further, unilateral practices by dominant firms having the object or possible effect of interfering with the market were also prohibited. Prohibited practices, however, could be exempted under Article 51(2) upon a showing that the practice furthered economic progress, particularly through increased productivity. A separate provision also prohibiting resale price maintenance was found in Article 37(4) of the Ordonnance of 30th June 1945, subject to possible exemption by ministerial order in the case of, inter alia, exclusive rights under a patent or licence.

Article 7 of the new ordonnance prohibits as before agreements which are aimed at or may have the effect of restraining or distorting competition. Specifically noted are agreements which may (1) limit market access or free competition by other firms, (2) restrain price movements, (3) limit output, investment or technical progress or (4) divide markets. Article 8 prohibits the abuse of a dominant position or of the economic dependence of a supplier or buyer. Abusive practices specifically identified under Article 8 include tied sales and sales under discriminatory provisions. Article 9 voids all contractual clauses which violate the terms of Articles 7 or 8.

The application of French competition law to intellectual property rights does not mean that those rights are not recognized. The need to reconcile the efficiency considerations of competition policy leads to the conclusion that the exercise of an intellectual property right is only abusive if that exercise restrains competition beyond that restraint inherent in protecting the right. The French competition authorities thus distinguish between the "existence" of an intellectual property right, which is not subject to competition law, and the "exercise" of that right, which does fall under competition law. Thus, only those licensing restrictions which are not inherent in the grant of an intellectual property right are subject to rules against anticompetitive practices. For example, practices seeking to extend the exclusivity of a patent beyond its term or to extend its reach would be subject to competition law.

French intellectual property law governs essentially the scope, origin and consequences of exclusive rights[14]. These laws do not regulate the economic exploitation of the rights confered but, in the case of non-use, the authorities can grant a compulsory licence. The law of 2nd January 1968 establishes three categories of such licences:(1) compulsory licences for non-use[15], (2) licences for blocking patents[16] and (3) licences as of right[17].

French competition authorities have not presumed that the grant of an intellectual property right establishes significant market power. In a recent opinion involving *agricultural chemicals*, discussed in detail in the next chapter, the Competition Commission found that patented pesticides faced sufficient interbrand competition that the ability to exercise market power was unlikely. Nonetheless, the particular restraint involved (resale price maintenance) was unlawful given the wording of Article 50, prohibiting agreements with the object of restricting competition; actual anticompetitive effects need not be shown. In this case, however, the Commission exonerated the agreement under Article 51 given its likely effect in promoting interbrand competition[18].

Germany

Patent and know-how licensing agreements are subject to Sections 20 and 21 of the Act against Restraints on Competition (ARC) to the extent that restrictions are placed on the licensee. Restrictions upon the licensor are governed by Sections 15 and 18 of the ARC while horizontal agreements, e.g. cross-licensing agreements or patent pools, are subject to Sections 1-8 of the ARC, dealing with cartels.

Section 20(1) provides that patent licensing agreements are void to the extent that they impose restrictions on the licensee which exceed the scope of the patent grant. Certain restrictions, however, are defined in Section 20(1) as not exceeding the patent right; the licensor can restrict the licence to certain uses, by the extent of his use or by quantity, territory or time. Additional exemptions are set forth in subsection 20(2), which permit restrictions to maintain quality, to maintain price, to exchange information and licence improvements, not to challenge the patent or to regulate competition outside Germany. Agreements prohibited under subsection 20(1) may be authorized by the Cartel Office under 20(3) if the "freedom of economic action of the acquirer or licensee or other enterprises is not unfairly restricted, and if competition in the market is not substantially restricted". Section 21 extends the treatment of Section 20 to legally unprotected know-how "as appropriate" and to the extent that the know-how constitutes a trade secret.

Restrictions on the licensor as to its pricing or dealings with third parties are null and void under Section 15. Section 18 authorizes the Cartel Office to void agreements, inter alia, restricting the licensor's sales to third parties where such restrictions are widespread, restrict entry by other firms or otherwise impair competition substantially.

Horizontal agreements by patentees or horizontal restrictions included in licensing agreements are void under Article 1 to the extent that they are arranged for a common purpose and are likely to restrain competition. Agreements may be authorised, however, under Sections 2-8 to the extent that particular conditions are fulfilled.

Given the increasing internationalisation of patenting and licensing, the effects of licensing agreements are now rarely restricted to the German domestic market. Where licensing agreements have effects not only within the Federal Republic but in the other EC Member states as well, they are also subject to European competition law. In such cases, the Federal Cartel Office (FCO) refers the parties to the agreement to the practice of the EC Commission in enforcing Article 85 of the Treaty of Rome. In many cases where licensing agreements clearly have cross-frontier effects, the enterprises involved usually turn directly to the EC Commission for the clarification of cartel-law problems. Therefore, the number of cases in which the FCO had to examine restrictions of competition in connection with licensing agreements has considerably declined over the past few years. The fact that the enterprises are largely familiar with the FCO's enforcement practice regarding Sections 20 and 21 of the ARC has also contributed to this development.

Where patent licensing agreements are void under Section 20, damages or a declaratory judgment can be obtained in a separate civil suit in appropriate circumstances. The cartel authority may prohibit the implementation of ineffective patent licensing agreements. Agreements specified in Sections 20 and 21 are not subject to a general notification requirement. However, agreements that are not included in the list of exempted agreements and therefore void without authorisation by the cartel authority have to be pre-notified. The last application under Section 20(3) was filed in 1974. Nevertheless, the FCO instituted a number of proceedings, either on the basis of its own investigations or in response to voluntary notifications that were filed for the sake of increased legal certainty by the enterprises concerned. The vast majority of proceedings were terminated without a formal decision, because the clauses challenged by the FCO were abandoned after informal talks with the FCO.

In addition, abuses of intellectual property rights by dominant enterprises are subject to Section 22 of the ARC according to which the FCO may invalidate abusive parts of contracts or issue cease and desist orders. It is established case law that a patent or another exclusive intellectual property right does not in itself constitute a dominant position the existence of which can only be determined by careful market analysis (see BGH, WuW 9/1973 - Bremsrollen).

Ireland

The Restrictive Practices Act, 1972, as amended in 1987, makes no mention of intellectual property rights or licensing as such. The Fair Trade Commission may hold an enquiry into the distribution of any kind of goods, or the provision of any service, with a view to determining whether these conditions involve restrictive practices or an interference with competition or trade which are unfair or operate against the common good. The Minister for Industry and Commerce may make an order prohibiting restrictive practices, unfair practices or unfair methods of competition. The Commission may also undertake studies and analyses of the effect on the common good of, inter alia, methods of competition and types of restrictive practice. Intellectual property rights have not been the subject of either an enquiry or study. Under the Patents Act, 1964, any person may apply to the Controller of Patents for a compulsory licence on the grounds that there has been an abuse of the monopoly rights under the patent, because, for example, the invention is not being commercially worked in the State.

Japan

Patent and know-how licensing practices are, with some exceptions, subject to the provisions of the Antimonopoly Act of 1947. An exception is set forth in Section 23 of that Act, which provides that the Antimonopoly Act does not apply to those acts which are "recognisable as the exercise of rights under ... the Patent Act ...". The Antimonopoly Act is applied only to licensing practices which are not recognized as an exercise of the patent rights, etc.

Licensing practices which are not recognised as an exercise of the patent rights, etc. could be subject to Section 3 of the Antimonopoly Act, which prohibits private monopolization and unreasonable restraint of trade. The first is defined as "business activities by which any entrepreneurs, individually or collectively, exclude or control the business activities of other entrepreneurs, thereby causing, contrary to the public interest, a substantial restraint of competition". Discriminatory pricing, exclusive dealing and controlling necessary resources for manufacturing or selling are among the methods used to effect "exclusion". Exclusive dealing, resale price maintenance and tie-in contracts are among the methods used for purposes of "control". The latter is defined as agreement or any other concerted action by which any entrepreneur with any other entrepreneur mutually restrict or conduct their business activities, thereby causing, contrary to the public interest, a substantial restraint of competition. Section 8 which prohibits unreasonable restraint of trade effected by a trade association could also be applicable to licensing practices which is not recognised as an exercise of the patent right, etc.

Licensing practices which are not recognized as an exercise of the patent right, etc. may also be reached under Section 19 of the Act, which prohibits "unfair trade practices". Unfair trade practices are defined as those which fall into certain categories, "tend to impede fair competition" and are designated as such by the Fair Trade Commission (FTC). Among the trade practices designated as unfair by the FTC are unjust tie-in, unjust exclusive dealing, unjust restriction on dealings between a customer-licensee and third parties and abuse of dominant bargaining position.

International licensing agreements receive separate attention under the Antimonopoly Act. Section 6(1) of the Act prohibits entrepreneurs from entering into an international agreement or contract which "contains such matters as constitute unreasonable restraint of trade or unfair trade practices". The FTC published Guidelines on 24th May 1968 identifying unfair trade practices in international patent and know-how introduction contracts. The Guidelines covered nine types of restrictions and identified certain acts considered to be the exercise of rights under the Patent Act and thereby exempted completely from the operation of the Antimonopoly Act under Section 23 discussed above.

In February 1989, the FTC published a revision of those Guidelines. The new Guidelines apply to both domestic and international licensing agreements and cover know-how transactions as well as patent licensing. The Guidelines relate only to possible unfair trade practices in violation of Section 19 of the Act and thus leave open the possibility that Section 3 of the Act as well as other provisions might also be applied in a particular case.

The new Guidelines create three categories of clauses: those which do not constitute unfair trade practices, those which may be unfair and those which are highly likely to be unfair. Cases falling into the middle category will be treated on a case-by-case basis following an examination which will take into account the position of the licensor and licensee in the relevant market, the conditions in that market and the duration of the restriction. For restrictions falling in the third category, there will be a presumption that the agreement is unfair unless the parties can present a specific justification for the restriction. The details of the Guidelines with respect to particular clauses will be presented in the next chapter.

Violations of Sections 3, 6, 8 or 19 of the Act may be the subject of cease and desist orders by the FTC. Further, violations under Sections 3, 6 or 8 could also be subject to criminal sanctions under Sections 89 and 90, including both fines and imprisonment, and courts hearing cases under these latter sections are empowered under Section 100 to revoke the offender's patent involved.

Netherlands

Dutch law and regulations have no specific rules dealing with competition aspects of intellectual property rights. Section 34 of the Dutch Patent Act, however, enables the Minister of Economic Affairs to impose a compulsory licence when necessary for the public interest. This provision of the Act, added in 1978, has not yet been applied. There is no definition for "public interest". The necessity of imposing a compulsory licence must be clarified in the light of all relevant circumstances.

Apart from the Patent Act, the Act on Economic Competition gives powers which might be used in relation to patents and patent licensing. Section 24 of this Act contains a special provision which the Minister of Economic Affairs may apply when there is a dominant position "whose consequences conflict with the public interest". Application of that paragraph is restricted to the use of the patent. Up to now Section 24 has not been applied in relation to patents or patent licences.

New Zealand

In New Zealand, intellectual property rights are established under five statutes - the Patents Act 1953, the Designs Act 1953, the Trade Mark Act 1953, the Copyright Act 1962 and the Plant Variety Rights Act 1987. To varying extents all these statutes provide for the granting of exclusive property rights for innovations in the relevant areas of endeavour. Most also provide an administrative regime for granting such rights including registration, term and transfer or assignment.

The Commerce Act 1986 is New Zealand's principal competition law. This Act seeks to promote competition in markets by, inter alia, prohibiting contracts arrangements or understandings which substantially lessen competition, collective boycotts, resale price maintenance, and the anticompetitive use of a dominant position in a market.

In relation to intellectual property the Commerce Act does not seek to interfere with the creation or legitimate exploitation of intellectual property rights. The Act provides that specific provisions of other statutes prevail. Furthermore specific exceptions in relation to intellectual property rights are provided in sections 36(2) and 45 of the Act.

Sections 27-30 of the Commerce Act prohibit contracts, arrangements or understandings which substantially lessen competition, are exclusionary or collectively fix prices. However, section 45 exempts from these provisions a contract, arrangement or understanding in relation to the use, licensing or assignment of intellectual property rights if:

  i)   it controls the nature, extent, territory, or period of the exercise of those rights or the type, quality, or quantity of goods or services to which those rights relate; or
  ii) it imposes restrictions for the purpose of protecting the interest of the owner, seller, or licensor in a technically satisfactory exploitation of those rights; or
  iii) it consists of an obligation on the part of the licensee or a party to the contract to exchange experience, or to grant licences for improvements in, or applied uses of, an invention, design, or plant variety, insofar as the obligation is identical to an obligation of another party who is an owner or seller or licensor of those rights; or
  iv) it consists of an obligation affecting competition in a market outside New Zealand, which obligation does not remain in force beyond the expiration of those rights.

Of course other provisions which extend beyond these exceptions remain subject to challenge.

Sections 37-42 of the Act prohibit resale price maintenance. Resale price maintenance in conjunction with patented goods or other intellectual property is not exempted from these general requirements.

Section 36 of the Act prohibits the use of a dominant position in a market for anticompetitive purposes. However, section 36(2) provides that a person cannot be held to have used a dominant position in a market for an anticompetitive purpose by reason only that that person enforced an intellectual property right. Other actions by dominant firms whether or not associated with intellectual property rights which had an anticompetitive purpose would however remain open to challenge under the Commerce Act.

No cases have yet been decided which have specifically addressed the interface between intellectual property and competition law. However some commentators have suggested the existing provisions of the Commerce Act in fact extend the scope of intellectual property. This was not the intention of the legislation and this issue has been identified for consideration during the recently commenced review of the Act's operation.

Portugal

Portugese law does not provide specifically for competition-related aspects of intellectual property licensing and relies instead on the general provisions of its competition law[19].

Article 13 of Portugese competition law forbids agreements having the object or effect of restraining competition while Article 14 prohibits abuse of dominant positions. Practices in violation of Articles 13 or 14 may nonetheless be permitted under Article 15, which exempts restrictive practices which improve productivity or distribution or promote economic or technical development, provided that consumers receive a fair share of the benefits, that the restrictions are indispensible to achieve the benefits and that the restrictions do not eliminate competition in a substantial part of the market.

Spain

Spanish competition policy can be applied to patent licensing practices. Further, Spanish patent law, the Law 11/86 on Patents and Utility Models, provides specifically for remedies in the case of anticompetitive licensing practices. Article 80, Chapter 11, Title 7 of that law provides that compulsory licenses can be ordered in the case of a violation of the Law 110/63 on Restrictive Business Practices. Even more recently, the Royal Decree 1750/87 of 18th December 1987 provides that anticompetitive clauses in matters relating to the transfer of technology will be presented to the Directorate General for the Protection of Competition[20].

Sweden

In Sweden intellectual property licensing agreements fall under the general provisions of Swedish competition legislation. This legislation is essentially based on the abuse principle. The Competition Ombudsman (NO) intervenes whenever he finds in a particular instance that some restrictive business practice has adverse economic effects. NO then negotiates to have these effects removed and, if necessary, may carry the case to the Market Court. The court may order the firm, under penalty of fine, to void the offending agreement or otherwise to desist from the restrictive practice. The only practices that are directly forbidden, and hence punishable, are resale price maintenance and collusive tendering.

Swedish competition law regards the protection that intellectual property offers as a restraint of trade per se, albeit of special nature given the goal of encouraging creative effort. Swedish intellectual property law consists mainly of rules about the origin, scope and meaning of sole and exclusive rights. The law does not regulate the economic exploitation of such rights except that the authorities may order compulsory licensing in certain instances of non-use.

In Swedish law the attitude towards the relationship between competition law and intellectual property has undergone a shift since the 1950s. It was then thought that competition law did not reach patent-related practices except when they were used to compel some other restraint of trade, for example by obligating resellers to charge a stated price[21]. In connection with later legislative matters[22] statements have been made which indicate broadened scope for competition law intervention in intellectual property matters. The legal picture was clarified when the Market Court handed down its ruling in the *Dubbman* case[23].

The *Dubbman* decision, discussed at greater length in the next chapter, established that Swedish competition law could be applied to even those terms of a patent licensing agreement which follow from the patent grant (here the quantity produced under the licence) where there are particularly serious anticompetitive effects. The test is whether the restraint of trade has a greater effect than is warranted under the intellectual property right.

The rule of the *Dubbman* case has been confirmed by subsequent developments. Statements contained in later government bills support the *Dubbman* rule[24] and legal scholars view *Dubbman* as establishing a precedent for intellectual property licensing generally[25].

Today's Competition Act is based on the findings of a commission of inquiry (*konkurrensutredningen*), published in the series of Government Official Reports[26]. The commission, making reference to the *Dubbman* case[27], wrote that the system then in effect afforded satisfactory scope, consistent with the aims of different regulations, for drawing limits to their application. In 1982, the legislature essentially endorsed the commission's interpretation of the relationship between competition law and intellectual property.

A further point to keep in mind is that under Swedish law intellectual rights are national, which means that the protection is restricted to the national territory. Thus, the Swedish legislation on intellectual property does not guard against the production, sale or importation abroad of a good or process protected in Sweden, nor against an outsider taking economic advantage abroad of such copying or imitation. However, imports into Sweden of such copies or imitations are covered by Swedish law and are prohibited, provided the Swedish rights holder has not consented to the imports.

In Sweden, parallel imports refer to the bringing into the country of a product, protected as intellectual property in whole or in part, from a country where it is produced by the rights owner or with the consent of said owner (the "genuine article"). In Sweden the legal position varies from one kind of right to another as regards the permissibility of parallel imports, mainly because such rights have differing protective aims.

Switzerland

In Switzerland, the law on cartels and similar organisations of 20th December 1985 applies only in a limited fashion to intellectual property licensing agreements. Thus anticompetitive effects stemming from the rights provided under industrial property or copyright legislation are not reached by the cartel law. The cartel law does apply, however, to licensing agreements involving a cartel or similar organisation if the licensing agreement restrains competition beyond the protection provided by statute.

United Kingdom

In the United Kingdom, patent and know-how licensing agreements may be subject in certain circumstances to the Fair Trading Act 1973, the Restrictive Trade Practices Act 1976 or the Competition Act 1980.

Under the Restrictive Trade Practices Act (RTP), an agreement between two or more parties doing business in the United Kingdom must be registered with the Director General of Fair Trading if more than one party accepts restrictions as to, inter alia, prices, terms, quantities or types of goods to be purchased or produced, territories or persons with whom he does business. Agreements which restrict only the licensee fall outside the terms of the Act. Unless the Secretary of State directs otherwise, all registered agreements are directed to the Restrictive Practices Court for review. A restrictive agreement is prohibited unless the Court finds that it operates in the public interest.

Otherwise registrable patent and know-how licensing agreements may escape the operation of the Restrictive Trade Practices Act in three main ways.

First, there are special provisions in Section 29 of the Act for the Secretary of State to exempt agreements which are important to the national economy. To qualify, the agreement must promote a project of substantial importance to the national economy, promote efficiency, be indispensible to achieve the project's goals, be no more restrictive than necessary and be in the national interest.

A second exemption is found in Schedule 3 to the Act, which exempts certain patent and know-how licensing agreements. Know-how agreements are exempted under Section 3 of Schedule 3 if there are no more than two parties to the agreement and any restrictions as set forth above relate only to the know-how which is the subject of the agreement or to the products produced thereby. Patent licensing agreements are exempted under Section 5 provided the restrictions are limited to the subject matter of the patent and the agreement does not involve patent pooling (agreements involving three or more parties each granting an interest in a patent or registered design).

Finally, there is the possibility that a court will not find certain form of licence agreement to involve a restraint of trade at all. Clauses in licences which restrict only the right acquired by the licensee are not regarded as restrictive under a long standing principle of the UK law on restraint of trade. The clauses are regarded as qualifications to the grant of the right, and are not restrictive because in the absence of the licence the licensee has no rights in respect of the subject matter of the licence. The licence can only improve his competitive position and by accepting what appear to be restrictions he loses no pre-existing freedom. The principle was applied to the 1976 Act, in the context of real property leases, in *Ravenseft Properties Limited's Application*[28].

Agreements which are exempt from the RTP Act may nevertheless be subject to the provisions of the Competition Act, whereby investigations may be carried out into anti-competitive practices. An anti-competitive practice is defined in the Act as a course of conduct pursued by a person in the course of business which "of itself or when taken together with a course of conduct pursued by persons associated with him, has or is intended or is likely to have the effect of restricting, distorting or preventing competition in connection with the production, supply or acquisition of goods in the United Kingdom or any part of it or the supply or securing of services in the United Kingdom or any part of it".

While restrictive licensing practices are reachable under the Competition Act, the Office of Fair Trading (OFT) has recently indicated that it will assess the practices on a case-by-case basis:

> "Some restriction of competition is inherent in the grant of any intellectual property right, the rationale being that invention, innovation and other creative activity will thereby be encouraged. A refusal to license such rights, is therefore fully compatible with the exercise of those rights. Nevertheless the effects of the restriction of competition may, in particular circumstances, and taking account of the market power of the firm enjoying the rights, be such as to suggest that a firm's licensing practices should be regarded as an anti-competitive practice. Similarly with the licensing of technology; while it cannot be suggested that a firm must be prepared to license its technology to all-comers there may be circumstances where a refusal to license so reinforces the market power of a firm that refusal should be regarded as anti-competitive."[29]

The other possible method of proceeding is under the Fair Trading Act. This Act is applicable to a firm exploiting a "monopoly situation" (a market share of 25 per cent or more). Investigations are conducted by the Monopolies and Mergers Commission (MMC) following a reference by the Director General of Fair Trading. The MMC determines whether the firm is acting to exploit or maintain its market power and, if so, whether those actions are against the public interest.

Where action taken under either the Competition Act or the Fair Trading Act results in a finding by the MMC that the practice operates against the public interest, the Secretary of State can use various orders making powers to remedy or prevent the adverse effects, or he can request the Director General to negotiate an undertaking. While neither fines nor interim injunctive relief are available, compulsory licensing is a possible remedy. Section 51 of the Patents Act 1977, as amended by Section 14 of the Competition Act, provides a procedure for the Secretary of State to seek a compulsory licence. Compulsory licences have been rarely sought however. According to a 1986 White Paper, "the consultations undertaken on the 1983 Green Paper have not produced any evidence to support the view that significant abuses of patent monopolies are going uncorrected. Indeed, the evidence points to the fact that little use is made of the compulsory licence provisions simply because there are very few relevant abuses of patent rights and that the owners of exploitable patents normally wish to work them to the fullest extent and/or license their use widely"[30].

United States

Patent and know-how licensing practices in the United States are subject to both public and private enforcement under the antitrust laws. In addition, defendants in infringement actions under the patent laws can assert "patent misuse" by the patentee as a defence. Conduct constituting patent misuse is similar but not necessarily identical to conduct violating the antitrust laws.

The applicable antitrust statutes are Section 1 of the Sherman Act, which prohibits contracts, combinations or conspiracies in unreasonable restraint of trade, and Section 2 of that Act, which prohibits monopolization and conspiracies and attempts to monopolize. Section 3 of the Clayton Act prohibits tie-in or exclusive dealing arrangements for goods "whether patented or unpatented" where the effect of the arrangement "may be to substantially lessen competition or tend to create a monopoly" in a market. Patent acquisition can further be attacked under Section 7 of the Clayton Act, which prohibits mergers and acquisitions, including the acquisition of assets, subject to the same anticompetitive effects requirement of Section 3 set out above.

Private parties can enforce these provisions and can obtain injunctions, treble damages, court costs and attorney's fees. Government enforcement is done by the Department of Justice (DOJ) and the Federal Trade Commission (FTC). The DOJ can seek injunctions, fines and criminal sanctions while the FTC, which enforces the standards of the Clayton and Sherman Acts through Section 5 of its own statute, can proceed in the federal courts for injunctions or issue cease and desist orders after administrative proceedings.

Although the application of the Sherman and Clayton Acts to patent and know-how licensing is developed in greater detail in the next chapter, some more general points are presented here. In particular, there is the special treatment which the competitive effects test of the Clayton Act receives when a patented (or copyrighted) good is involved. The doctrine which has developed is that as long as some "quantitatively significant" sales volume is involved, a licensing restriction within Section 3 amounts to a per se violation when the good is patented or copyrighted[31]. While lower courts have begun to question whether market power should be presumed merely from the fact of a patent[32], that view is not yet clearly established in the Supreme Court. In *Walker Process Equipment v. Food Machinery and Chemical Corporation*[33], an infringement action in which the defendant counter-claimed under Section 2 that the plaintiff was monopolizing through the use of a fraudulently obtained patent, the Supreme Court held that it was "necessary to appraise the exclusionary power of the illegal patent claim in terms of the relevant market for the product"[34]. Later, however, in *Jefferson Parish*, a tying or exclusive dealing case not involving intellectual property, the majority opinion (joined in by five justices) recited earlier decisions finding anticompetitive forcing likely, and therefore per se illegal, where "the Government has granted the seller a patent or similar monopoly over a product"[35]. Four other justices concurred in the result but took issue with the majority's treatment of tie-ins. Relevant at this point is the concurring opinion's criticism of using a patent as a proxy for market power:

> "a common misconception has been that a patent or copyright, a high market share, or a unique product that competitors are not able to offer suffices to demonstrate market power. While each of these three factors might help to give market power to a seller, it is

42

also possible that a seller in these situations will have no market power: for example, a patent holder has no market power in any relevant sense if there are close substitutes for the patented product"[36].

Another point which can be considered here is that antitrust analysis of patent licensing in the US has been shaped by provisions of the Patent Act and cases thereunder. Three particular principles stand out. First, the patentee is under no duty to exploit his invention. He can restrain others from using it even if he does not do so himself[37]. (While compulsory licensing may be a remedy in patent litigation, it stems from the courts' equitable powers rather than from a duty to exploit inventions.) Second, the patent grant implies the right of the patentee to issue restrictive licences. The Patent Act provides that licensees may be restricted, e.g. to particular uses or territories within the United States[38]. This express recognition of the patentee's right to issue restrictive licences is reflected in the cases developed in the next chapter. Third, the powers of the patentee to create such restrictions end with the sale of the patented article; the patentee may restrict his licensee but his rights are exhausted by the first sale of the article either by him or his licensee[39].

The general principles set out above have helped to shape both the application of the antitrust laws to licensing practices and the doctrine of patent misuse, the doctrine available to parties seeking to defend against an action for infringement. Briefly, courts will refuse to enforce a patent against an infringer if the patentee is found to have misused his grant and the effects of that misuse have not been corrected. Misuse can be found either if there is (1) an antitrust violation sufficiently related to the patent or (2) an attempt to "extend" the patent monopoly[40]. Conduct penalized under the patent extension doctrine is similar to conduct regulated under the antitrust laws, a tie-in, for example, can constitute misuse. Under the misuse doctrine there is no requirement that there be an anticompetitive effect from the "extension". What results is a per se rule for conduct which may or may not be found to violate the antitrust laws.

The current Administration has proposed legislation which would bring patent misuse within the confines of antitrust doctrine. Legislation proposed in the Omnibus Intellectual Property Rights Improvement Act of 1987 would amend the doctrine of patent misuse by making it unavailable against certain conduct unless that conduct also violated the antitrust laws[41].

The Act would further amend the antitrust standard to be applied to intellectual property licensing. Section 3102 (a) of the Act would require a rule of reason standard to be applied to all antitrust actions concerning patent, know-how or copyright licensing. Section 3102 (b) would eliminate treble damages in such suits, providing instead for actual damages plus costs and attorney's fees. Section 3106 (a) would codify certain rules for the operation of no-challenge clauses and is dealt with in the next chapter.

Finally, two recent sets of guidelines published by the Department of Justice are relevant as official statements of the Department's reading of the law and its enforcement policy. DOJ published in 1985 its *Vertical Restraints Guidelines* which outlined its view of the law of non-price vertical restraints. Although the analysis of the Guidelines expressly does not apply to intellectual property licensing, it is relevant nonetheless as antitrust rules for intellectual property licensing follow from antitrust analysis applied generally to horizontal or vertical restraints. The Guidelines state:

"These Guidelines also do not apply to restrictions in licences of intellectual property (e.g., patent, a copyright, trade secret, and know-how). Such restrictions often are essential to ensure that new technology realizes its maximum legitimate return and benefits consumers as quickly and efficiently as possible. Moreover, intellectual property licences often involve the co-ordination of complementary, not competing, inputs. Thus, a rule of reason analysis is appropriate. Unless restrictions in intellectual property licences involve naked restraints of trade unrelated to development of the intellectual property, or are used to co-ordinate a cartel among the owners of competing intellectual properties, or suppress the creation of development of competing intellectual properties, the restrictions should not be condemned. However, because the anticompetitive risks and the procompetitive benefits of restrictions in licences are somewhat different from the potential of typical vertical restraints, the rule of reason analysis may also differ from (and be even more lenient than) that set out in these Guidelines."[42]

The DOJ's new *Antitrust Enforcement Guidelines for International Operations* (DOJ Guidelines) describe the DOJ's current competitive analysis of intellectual property licensing agreements[43]. Although the DOJ's analysis is set forth in the context of international licensing arrangements, the Guidelines state that the same analysis applies to purely domestic licensing arrangements as well. This chapter briefly describes the general analysis set forth in the DOJ Guidelines. Treatment of specific types of licensing practices is discussed in Chapter 5. The basic premise of the DOJ Guidelines is that the creation, transfer, and licensing of intellectual property should be analysed in the same way that the DOJ analyses the creation and transfer of any other form of tangible or intangible property and that the owner of intellectual property is fully entitled to exploit any market power which is inherent in the property itself. According to the DOJ Guidelines:

"The owner of intellectual property is fully entitled to enjoy whatever market power the property itself may confer. Indeed, respecting the rights of the creator of intellectual property to enjoy the full value of that property provides the incentive for the innovative effort required to create the property. And the results of that innovative effort both increase productive efficiency and expand society's knowledge and wealth."[44]

The Guidelines further indicate that restraints in intellectual property licences "can play an important role in ensuring that new technology realizes its maximum return and benefits consumers as quickly and efficiently as possible"[45].

The DOJ has no list of approved licence restrictions. The DOJ Guidelines state that the DOJ analyzes restrictions in an intellectual property licence under a rule of reason except where the underlying transfer is a sham (that is, where the parties demonstrably are not interested in conveying and receiving intellectual property rights, but are using the licence to disguise an effort to restrict output or raise price in some market other than the market for the intellectual property). Sham licensing arrangements intended to fix the price or output of technology or some other product may be subject to criminal prosecution as per se unlawful. Under a rule of reason the DOJ will challenge a licensing arrangement only if *(i)* the arrangement would likely create, enhance, or facilitate the exercise of market power beyond that which is inherent in the intellectual property itself and *(ii)* the risk of anticompetitive harms is not outweighed by procompetitive efficiencies that would result from the arrangement. The DOJ will not challenge a licensing arrangement unless it would have a significant anticompetitive effect, regardless of whether the arrangement actually would generate procompetitive efficiencies[46]. The DOJ considers the cumulative anticompetitive risks and procompetitive benefits of a licensing arrangement, and does not attempt to assign and balance the risks and benefits of particular features of a licence. Nevertheless, if a particular licensing restriction that would have an anticompetitive effect is not related to achieving any efficiencies claimed by the parties, the DOJ will likely require the restriction to be stricken[47].

The DOJ Guidelines distinguish between agreements that merely exploit the market power inherent in an innovation and those that create, enhance, or facilitate the exercise of market power by *(i)* restraining competition that does or would exist in the absence of the licence or *(ii)* excluding competing technologies or products from a relevant market.

The DOJ's rule-of-reason analysis of intellectual property licensing arrangements involves four steps. The first three steps are designed to determine whether the licence would likely have an anticompetitive effect in any relevant market. Step 1 focuses on anticompetitive effects in a relevant technology market. Step 2 focuses on anticompetitive effects in markets for products that incorporate the licensed technology and in markets where no license integration occurs. Step 3 focuses on anticompetitive effects resulting from vertical restraints that may not have been examined under steps 1 and 2. Finally, in Step 4, the DOJ determines whether any risk of anticompetitive effects detected under the first three steps is outweighed by procompetitive efficiencies[48].

EEC

Intellectual property licensing agreements in the EEC are subject to Article 85 of the Treaty of Rome, the basic provision governing anti-competitive agreements, and to regulations promulgated thereunder. Article 85 is broad enough to capture the licensing practices examined in this report, but Article 86 could also be applied as well. Article 86, which governs abuse of dominant positions, conceivably could be applied to unilateral licensing conduct, e.g. a refusal to license.

Article 85(1) prohibits all agreements "which may affect trade between Member States" and which have as their object or effect the prevention, restriction or distortion of competition within the common market. Prohibited provisions are automatically void under Article 85(2) unless exempted by the Commission under Article 85(3).

Article 85(3) is particularly relevant to intellectual property licensing agreements. It permits agreements to be exempted from 85(1) which contribute "to improving the production or distribution of goods or to promoting technical or economic progress". Such agreements, however, must provide consumers a "fair share" of their resulting advantages and impose only those restrictions which are "indispensable" to the success of the agreement. Further, the agreement must not create the "possibility of eliminating competition in respect of a substantial part of the products in question".

A licensing agreement can also be found not to offend 85(1) at all if the Commission grants a "negative clearance" with respect to a notified agreement. A negative clearance for an agreement, finding it not to be a restrictive agreement within 85(1), means that the Commission does not need to consider whether the agreement can be exempted under 85(3).

The application of Article 85 to licensing agreements is complicated by other articles in the Treaty of Rome relating to the free movement of goods and to the protection of national intellectual property rights. In particular, Articles 30 and 34, aimed at market integration, prohibit quantitative restrictions on imports or exports between Member countries. On the other hand, Article 36 of the Treaty expressly preserves national intellectual property rights, including the right to block infringing imports. The Court of Justice has reconciled the goals of competition and market integration with the preservation of national intellectual property rights by finding that the "existence" of a right was preserved under the Treaty but that the "exercise" of the right could still be regulated[49].

The interaction between Article 85 and these other articles relating specifically to intellectual property rights is developed in a number of decisions by the Court of Justice and the EC Commission. These decisions are discussed in the next chapter according to their specific subject matter.

More recently, the Commission has issued two block exemptions related to intellectual property licensing. The first, issued on 23rd July 1984, relates to patent licensing practices[50]. The second relates to know-how licensing[51]. "Know-how" is defined in the latter regulation as "a body of technical information that is secret, substantial and identified in any appropriate form"[52]. Both regulations follow the same pattern: Article 1 of each regulation identifies obligations in licensing agreements which are exempted under Article 85(3) from the operation of Article 85(1). The benefits of Article 1, however, apply only to agreements limited to two parties; agreements between three or more parties fall outside Article 1 completely. Article 2 of each regulation identifies additional obligations which are "generally not restrictive of competition". This article operates, in effect, as a kind of negative clearance decision for the clauses identified therein. Article 3 of each regulation sets forth prohibited clauses. Article 3 operates by denying the benefits of Article 1 and 2 to agreements which contain any of the clauses listed in Article 3. Article 4 provides for clauses neither exempted by Articles 1 and 2 nor prohibited by Article 3. Agreements containing such clauses will be exempted provided that the agreement is notified to the Commission and that the Commission does not oppose the agreement within six months. Article 5 states that the regulation does not apply to patent or know-how pools, to agreements related to joint ventures, to reciprocal licensing agreements, to the licensing of plant breeders' rights (in the patent licensing regulation) or to certain licensing agreements involving copyright, design rights or software (in the know-how regulation). Finally, Article 9 of each regulation reserves for the Commission the right to withdraw the benefits of the regulation in particular cases. The Commission identifies here a number of circumstances where the regulation might be withdrawn, including cases where the licensed product is "not exposed to effective competition" in the relevant market and cases where either party acts to impede parallel importers, e.g. by refusing to supply orders coming from parallel importers or from users outside the licensed area.

The patent licensing block exemption applies both to "pure" patent licensing agreements and to "mixed" agreements which include an element of know-how. However, if patents are not necessary for the achievement of the objects of the technology or the agreement contains obligations which restrict the exploitation of the relevant technology in Member States without patent protection, the agreement is governed by the know-how regulation.

The two regulations do differ in important aspects stemming from the non-public and unprotected nature of know-how. To protect against cartel agreements in the guise of know-how licences, the know-how regulation requires that the know-how transfered be "substantial" and that it be committed to writing. Further, because the life of know-how is not limited by legislation, the regulation puts time limits on the life of certain terms.

DISCUSSION

It might be useful to consider at this point how some of the major features of competition policy regimes interact with intellectual property licensing arrangements, particularly licensing arrangements which work in an essentially vertical fashion. This report argued in Chapter 3 that restrictions in such vertical agreements likely served a variety of procompetitive ends, such as creating incentives for a licensee to invest in and promote a new technology, lowering price for cost-sensitive consumers and reducing risk and transaction costs. Further, unless certain market conditions are present, there is little risk that such restraints will have anticompetitive effects; rather, the restraints are likely to be procompetitive and to provide a boost to interbrand competition.

The potential procompetitive effects of certain vertical restraints in IPR licensing agreements are not, however, reflected in the structure of some of the competition laws and policies surveyed in this chapter. For example, in some jurisdictions, as in France or the EEC, the relevant provisions seem aimed at preventing cartels as they prohibit all agreements with the object or effect of restraining trade. Such provisions work well in a horizontal context but less so when applied vertically, for if read too literally they would outlaw "restrictive agreements" on an intrabrand level which serve to promote interbrand competition. Further, the exemption possibilities from these prohibitions, generally requiring a showing that the restraint is "indispensible" and that benefits are fairly shared with consumers, seem again better suited to cartel arrangements than to vertical licensing agreements. Here the burden falls on the licensor to prove that a restraint is necessary when such proof may be very difficult to come by. Second, where vertical restraints are aimed at helping an innovator capture the surplus created by the innovation and given the incentive to innovate which those rents create, it does not seem logical to require a showing that a "fair share" is *not* being appropriated.

Given the problems raised by prohibition-oriented competition policies for vertical type restraints in licensing agreements, the efforts by the EC Commission at patent and know-how block exemptions take on considerable importance by creating some areas of legal certainty where licensors can impose restraints. As will be seen in the next chapter, however, the areas covered by the block exemption are somewhat more narrow than the range of procompetitive vertical restraints, a difficulty inherent in trying to deal by regulation with provisions which have to be evaluated on a case-by-case basis balancing pro- and anticompetitive effects.

On the other hand, looking at one "rule of reason" jurisdiction, the United States provides an example of how a competition law framed for balancing the pro- and anticompetitive effects in vertical licensing arrangement can yield unsatisfactory results if the analysis is based on questionable assumptions There, for example, courts have developed the presumption of market power in the patent context, distorting analysis of licensing agreements, especially when that presumption is combined with theories of "monopoly extension" or "leveraging" of the assumed monopoly. Likewise, the development of the effectively per se equitable doctrine of patent misuse and its use by private litigants may frustrate efforts by competition officials to weigh pro- and anticompetitive effects of licensing agreements before bringing an enforcement action. Thus the recently published Department of Justice Guidelines provide a useful framework for analysis but their impact on private actions is uncertain unless the patent misuse doctrine is modified legislatively.

This discussion has focused on jurisdictions which will figure prominently in the following chapter, where particular cases are taken up. Given the difficulties in some of the

47

regulatory frameworks pointed up here, the method of analysis used in those cases is particularly important if those licensing agreements which are likely to operate procompetitively are not to be unnecessarily prohibited.

Chapter 5

THE APPLICATION OF COMPETITION POLICY
TO LICENSING AGREEMENTS

This chapter discusses the application of competition laws and policies in cases involving the licensing of patents or know-how. This discussion will be organised along the lines of the major clauses which parties may seek to include in such agreements. These clauses generally relate to prices, quantities, territories, exclusivity, fields of use, tie-ins, package licensing, the imposition of royalties on unpatented products or on total sales, the granting back of improvements or prohibitions on challenges by the licensee. Cross-licensing or patent pooling may involve many of these topics but is treated separately given the particular risk of cartelization posed by such agreements. Also included are cases involving refusals to license and cases dealing with patent acquisitions. The cases, of course, often involve more than one type of clause, and thus may reappear at several points in the discussion below. Also included in the discussion are relevant regulations and statements of administrative guidance where such documents are organised by licensing clause. Such regulations and guidelines have been published, as noted in the previous chapter, by the EC Commission, the Fair Trade Commission of Japan and the US Department of Justice.

A. PRICING AGREEMENTS

France

In 1983 the Competition Commission issued an opinion related to practices in the market for *agricultural chemicals*[1]. The matter involved a number of manufacturers who had, inter alia, sought to fix prices and product lines. Some of the products were not patented while others were protected by either patents or other industrial property rights.

Products involving the herbicide triazine were the subject of price-fixing efforts by Ciba-Geigy in the late 1970s. Ciba's triazine patent had expired in 1975 and in 1978 it met with Agrishell in an effort to raise the price of Agrishell compounds utilizing triazine. In 1978 and 1979, Ciba met with the firms Procida, Prochim, Fisons Pepro and Agrishell in a further effort to maintain unit prices of triazine which included the sharing of pricing information. The Commission found, however, that these efforts were unsuccessful given the competition in triazines provided by still other firms.

The product Isoproturon was the subject of cartel efforts in 1979 by the firm Rhône-Poulenc Agrochimie, which held certain industrial property rights in the product. In particular, Rhône-Poulenc tried to organize firms using that compound to direct their efforts to the sale of more expensive products using Isoproturon in conjunction with other chemicals rather than the sale of pure Isoproturon. The Commission found that these efforts were partially successful; pure Isoproturon remained on the market but only in modest quantities. (The opinion does not indicate whether there were substitutes for Isoproturon-based products.)

Three patented products, Bellater, Primagarde and Avadex, were the subject of co-distribution agreements between their respective patentees (or the French licensees of patentee Monsanto in the case of Avadex) and other firms which involved price-fixing and the co-ordination of marketing strategies. Thus, Agrishell, Ciba-Geigy and Procida arranged the sale of Bellater and Primagarde while Rhodiagri and CFB (BASF) co-ordinated the distribution of Avadex. The Commission found, however, that each product faced sufficient competition from substitutes that the firms lacked power to raise price without conspiring with these additional competitors. Such conspiracies were neither alleged nor shown to exist. Thus, Avadex prices dropped significantly in spite of the price-fixing agreement given competition from substitute products. Likewise, Agrishell's products Bellater and Prima-garde faced competition from dozens of products, leading the firm to eventually abandon the co-distribution in an effort to increase the profitability of its products.

The Commission's opinion found that each of these agreements fell within the prohibition of Article 50 of the Ordinance of 30th June 1945, as each had at least the objective of restraining competition; actual anticompetitive effects need not be shown for Article 50 to be violated. The Commission then went on to consider whether the agreements could be exempted under Article 51, second sub-paragraph, as measures to increase economic progress.

The co-distribution agreements related to the patented products Bellater, Primagarde and Avadex were found to qualify under Article 51, as the co-distribution measures served to increase the presence of the products in the market place, increasing competition. This increased interbrand competition was found to outweigh the slight decrease in intrabrand competition caused by the price restraints.

In contrast, Ciba-Geigy's efforts to fix prices on its off-patent triazines were denied the benefits of Article 51; the period of patent protection was seen as the reward for the economic progress brought to agriculture by the invention of triazines. Ciba-Geigy's efforts to fix prices once the product was off-patent was seen as aggravating its offence under Article 50, although its co-conspirators were not found to be similarly guilty of overreaching.

The efforts of Rhône-Poulenc to control prices and formulations of Isoproturon products were likewise found to violate Article 50 and not to benefit from Article 51. Even though Isoproturon was covered by industrial property rights (the opinion does not specify the nature of the rights), the restrictive practices did not benefit from Article 51. Apparently, an affirmative showing must be made, as in the case of the co-distribution arrangements discussed above, that the restriction promotes economic progress.

The Commission, having found these various violations of Article 50 as well as further violations relating to efforts to discipline a discounting distributor, assessed penalties totalling 7.3 million francs, of which 2 million were assigned to Ciba-Geigy, apparently for its conduct concerning its off-patent product.

Germany

In the *Bremsrollen* case decided in 1973 the Federal Court had to evaluate the validity under German competition law of mutual price restrictions agreed upon between a licensor and a licensee[2].

The plaintiff, who had invented a braking device for conveyor belts and filed for patent protection in several West European countries, concluded a licensing agreement with the defendant granting him the exclusive right to sell the product at a minimum fixed price in a number of European countries. According to the terms of the agreement, the defendant was precluded from selling the product in Germany but on his part the plaintiff undertook to respect the agreed minimum price for his own sales on the German market. The parties agreed on a lump sum royalty fee of which only a part was paid. Subsequently, the defendant questioned the value of the invention, considered the contract to be invalid and refused to pay the remainder of the fee.

A crucial element for the decision was the Court's interpretation of the scope of Section 20 of the German Act against Restraints of Competition (ARC) and the relationship between this section and other provisions of the Act dealing with vertical restraints. Section 20 provides that restrictions extending beyond the scope of the protected interest are invalid under the Act but specifically exempts from the prohibition certain types of clauses including price obligations imposed on the licensee. According to well established case law, Section 20 is applicable even if a patent is not yet finally granted because the inventor has a legitimate interest to license pending the patent application. However, the exemptions provided in Section 20(2) has to be narrowly construed and even by invoking the principle of good faith cannot be extended to apply to price restrictions agreed upon by the licensor.

In the view of the Court, the rationale for allowing price restraints on the licensee is the licensor's recognised interest in influencing the pricing of the patented product either because the end price serves as a basis for computing the license fee or because he wants to prevent the licensee from competing by means of unpatented but similar products at inferior prices. The Court recognised that the licensee too may have an interest to impose price restrictions on the licensor either concerning his own sales activities or the licensing agreements to be concluded with third parties in particular if the licensee has taken the risk of introducing the product in important segments of the market. However, the Court concludes that this interest is not protected by the specific exemption provided under Section 20(2) and that therefore the general provisions of the Act banning horizontal or vertical price-fixing apply. It is only in special circumstances that a licensee, according to the principle of good faith, can adjust his own pricing policies to those of the licensor if otherwise any reasonable exploitation of the license as envisaged in the contract would become impossible.

Japan

In the *Yakult Co.* case in 1965, the FTC held that resale price maintenance and restriction of retailers' sales areas by the licensor, Yakult Co., was not recognized as an exercise of patent and trademark rights. Yakult had the process patent rights for manufacturing fermented milk and the trademark rights for the name "Yakult", which enjoyed a dominant position in the fermented milk producing market. Under the patent and trademark licensing agreements between Yakult and its bottlers, the company sold the syrup to the bottlers who then, after diluting and bottling, sold the final products to retailers. These

51

agreements included certain clauses in order to enable Yakult to effectively control the distribution channel. In particular, the bottlers would sell the products only to those retailers who had agreed with Yakult to observe the retail price, sales area and quantity designated by Yakult and not to sell competing products. Further, the bottlers would force the retailers to observe the retail price and sales area. The FTC decided that the restrictions in these two clauses were not recognized as an exercise of patent and trademark rights, that the company violated Section 19 (unfair trade practices) and ordered Yakult Co. to delete the clauses.

More recently, in 1982, the FTC issued a warning against concerned actions involving misuse of patent rights by pharmaceutical companies. Since 1965 *Fujisawa Pharmaceutical Co.* had been manufacturing metochroplamide (a medication used for digestive difficulties) under an exclusive patent licensing agreement with a French company, SECIF (Société d'Etudes Scientifiques et Industrielles de l'Ile de France). In 1971, three other Japanese companies - Yamanouchi Pharmaceutical Co., Nippon Kayaku Co. and Teikoku Chemical Industrial Co. - started to manufacture the same medication using their own patented production method. Having indicated that the production method employed by the three companies might infringe upon the patent of SECIF, Fujisawa proposed that, rather than going to court, the three companies reach an agreement with Fujisawa. As a result, an agreement was concluded under which Fujisawa and the three companies agreed not to bring any court action under the Patent Act with regard to the production and the sale of metochroplamide. In addition, the three companies would pay seven per cent of their sales revenue from the medication to Fujisawa as a "respect fee". Further, Fujisawa and the three companies agreed to co-operate to block new entries into the market as much as possible. The patents established thereafter by all three companies would be in joint ownership with SECIF or Fujisawa and the three companies agreed never to license any third party to use the patents nor sell materials to produce metochroplamide. Finally, Fujisawa and the three companies would co-operate to stabilise the market by observing the minimum sale price and market share which were listed in the annex to the agreements. The FTC noted in a warning to all four companies that these practices were not recognized as an exercise of patent rights and might violate Section 3 of the Act [private monopolisation and unreasonable restraint of trade (cartels)].

In its recent Guidelines on Unfair Trade Practices with respect to Patent and Know-How licensing Agreements, the FTC has stated that price agreements could, depending on the circumstances, fall into any of the three categories it has established for reviewing licensing agreements (agreements that are not unfair, that may be unfair or that are highly likely to be unfair). Licensing agreements involving either patents or know-how which would set the price or resale price of the licensed item in Japan would be considered to be highly likely to be unfair. On the other hand, agreements fixing export prices would not be found to be unfair where either *(a)* the licensor has registered a patent covering the technology in the export market, *(b)* the licensor has been continuously marketing the item in that market or *(c)* the licensor assigns that market exclusively to a third party. If conditions *(a)*, *(b)* and *(c)* are absent, the Guidelines state that an agreement setting export prices may be found to be unfair after case-by-case analysis.

Sweden

In Sweden, the *Dubbman* decision is the leading case on the permissibility of price restraints in patent licensing agreements[3]. *Dubbman* involved a licence between two manufacturers of tyre studs which accounted for 92 per cent of the Swedish market. This agreement provided for the licensor and licensee to charge uniform prices and allocated quotas to each firm. With respect to the price provision, the Market Court found that the rights granted under patent law did not include the power to set licensee prices. Further, as the price restraint was harmful, it was disallowed. This approach was later followed in the matter of *GKN Screws and Fasteners Ltd (England)*, as that company had licensed the Swedish firm AB Bahco Verktyg with respect to certain patented screwdrivers. Following NO's intervention, the parties deleted a clause related to resale price maintenance.

United States

In the United States, the competition rules applicable to price restrictions for patented products can be traced through a series of Supreme Court decisions going back at least 60 years. These decisions should be considered, however, in light of developments in the resale price maintenance doctrine as it applies to non-patented products. A very recent Supreme Court decision presented at the end of this section may well modify the rules for patented products as well.

A good starting point is the Court's 1926 decision in *United States v. General Electric Co.*[4], an appeal by the government for an injunction against further violation of the Sherman Act by General Electric (GE) for two alleged types of price-fixing violations related to the sale of its patented lightbulbs. One alleged violation related to efforts to control the resale prices of bulbs manufactured by GE. The Court found that the legal device used by GE in its distribution system - consignment sales through its agents - avoided an intermediate sale of the item which would otherwise bar setting the retail price, resale price maintenance being per se unlawful[5].

The second alleged violation concerned GE's efforts to control the retail prices of bulbs manufactured by Westinghouse, its only licensee, which used the same agency-style distribution network as GE. The Court reasoned from the powers inherent in the patent grant to restrict assignees and licensees:

> "The owner of a patent may assign it to another and convey (1) the exclusive right to make, use and vend the invention throughout the United States or (2) an undivided part or share of that exclusive right or (3) the exclusive right under the patent within and through a specific part of the United States. But any assignment or transfer short of one of these is a license giving the licensee no title in the patent and no right to sue at law in his own name for an infringement. Conveying less than title to the patent or part of it, the patentee may grant a licence to make, use and vend articles under the specifications of his patent for any royalty or upon any condition the performance of which is reasonably within the reward which the patentee by the grant of the patent is entitled to secure."[6]

Since a patentee could limit a licensee to the manufacture of the patented time for its own use but not for sale to others, it followed that price restrictions could be placed on licences to sell, "provided the conditions of sale are normally and reasonably adopted to secure pecuniary reward for the patentee's monopoly"[7]. The Court found it reasonable for a patentee to seek to control a licensee's prices in order to preserve the profitability of its own business[8].

A contrary result can be found in *United States v. Univis Lens Co.*[9], decided fifteen years after *General Electric*. In that case, Univis lens manufactured patented eyeglass lens blanks which it sold to wholesalers and "finishing retailers" and through them to prescription retailers, all of whom were licensees. Univis sought to control the price of its lenses at each level of distribution, including the final retail price of completed lenses. The district court found that the wholesalers and finishing retailers who ground and polished the rough lens blanks were practising the patent and thus subject to price restrictions under *General Electric*, while exhaustion occurred on the sale of finished lenses to retailers. The Supreme Court disagreed, finding that the wholesalers and finishers also should not be subject to price restraints. The Court found a right to process the blank into a finished lens inherent in the sale of the blank. Thus Univis exhausted its patent rights on the first sale of its lenses and subsequent attempts to impose price restraints were unlawful under Section 1 of the Sherman Act.

Six years after *Univis*, the Court took up the question of resale price maintenance in the context of a cross-licensing agreement between holders of mutually blocking patents. In that case, *United States v. Line Material Co.*[10], the government sought to enjoin alleged violations of Section 1 of the Sherman Act. The two principal defendants, Line Material and Southern States Electrical, held interfering patents on a type of electrical fuse. Southern States held the dominant patent while Line held an improvement patent; full exploitation of the device thus required rights to practise both patents. Initially, the firms cross-licensed each other and Line further granted Southern exclusive rights to sub-license the Line improvement. While the cross-licensing arrangement was royalty-free, the parties agreed to share sub-licensing income. Further, Line agreed to follow Southern's prices with respect to this particular product and Southern's sub-licensing agreements included a provision restricting licensees to follow Southern's prices. Southern thus was in a position to dictate prices for all firms which manufactured the patented fuse. (All manufacturers of fuses of this type evidently were licensed and the patented item accounted for about 41 per cent of their production.) The district court dismissed the charges, finding the pricing restrictions lawful under the *General Electric* case discussed above.

The government urged the Supreme Court to reverse and to overrule *General Electric*. The Court, however, found that it had neither a majority to overrule *General Electric* nor a majority to reaffirm it. What it did instead was to distinguish *Line Material* on the basis of the cross-licensing aspect, finding a per se unlawful agreement to fix prices in the agreement between Line and Southern. Thus, even though the patents were blocking, the Court held that "when patentees join in an agreement as here to maintain prices on their several products, that agreement, however advantageous it may be to stimulate the broader use of patents, is unlawful per se under the Sherman Act"[11].

On the same day that *Line Material* was decided, the Supreme Court issued its opinion in *United States v. United States Gypsum Co.*[12], which focused on price-fixing between a single patentee and numerous licensees. In *Gypsum*, the product was patented closed-edge wallboard, a product which outperformed and cost less to manufacture than unpatented open-edge wallboard. US Gypsum, holder of the original as well as subsequent patents on closed-edge board, established licensing agreements with almost all other gypsum board manufacturers which set prices of both patented and unpatented board and further established various terms of sale and distribution, e.g. the use of basing point pricing by all parties.

The district court dismissed the government's case, finding that the evidence did not establish a violation of Sections 1 and 2 of the Sherman Act under *General Electric*. The Supreme Court reversed, finding that, as it had in *Line Material*, that "conspiracies to control prices and distribution" were beyond "any patent privilege"[13]. The Court's opinion examined at some length the evidence which tended to show a conspiracy to restrain trade in this market. This evidence included the use of identical licensing agreements, the knowledge of each licensee that its competitors were subscribing to the same terms, the expressed unwillingness of some firms to join in unless the others went along, the agreements as to the price of unpatented board to preserve the stability of the cartel and the willingness of licensees to sign new agreements on an improvement of doubtful merit ("bubble board" - board manufactured with gypsum lightened by soap bubbles) in order to gain an additional 17 years of price stability. In short, the evidence tended to show that in this case one firm's patents were being used to effectuate a horizontal conspiracy among the patentee's competitor/licensees, and the Court was unwilling to permit patent law to legitamize price-fixing which would otherwise constitute a per se violation of the Sherman Act.

More recent decisions by the Supreme Court show how resale price maintenance agreements are currently treated when the arrangement is truly vertical in nature. These decisions, *Monsanto Co. v. Spray-Rite Service Co.*[14] and *Business Electronics Corp. v. Sharp Electronics Corp.*[15], both relate to resale price maintenance in the context of distribution relationships rather than licensor/licensee relationships, but nonetheless likely indicate how the Court would decide a similar issue in the patent or know-how licensing context.

In *Monsanto*, Spray-Rite, a large-volume, low-margin operator, alleged a conspiracy between Monsanto and other distributors to fix resale prices of Monsanto products. Monsanto, on the other hand, claimed that it terminated Spray-Rite because it failed to hire trained salesmen and promote sales sufficiently. Thus the plaintiff characterized the events as involving concerted vertical price fixing, still per se unlawful, while the defendant portrayed the situation as involving non-price vertical restraints, subject to the rule of reason under *Continental T.V. Inc. v. GTE Sylvania Inc.*[16]. The Department of Justice intervened as amicus curiae and argued that the rule of reason should apply to resale price maintenance. While the Court ultimately did not reach that issue and affirmed both the judgement against Monsanto (including a $10.5 million treble damage award) and the per se rule against conspiracies to fix resale prices, it showed considerable sympathy for efforts by the manufacturer to control resale prices:

> "The economic effect of all of the conduct described above - unilateral and concerted vertical price setting, agreements on price and nonprice restrictions - is in many, but not all, cases similar or identical. ... It is precisely in cases in which the manufacturer attempts to further a particular marketing strategy by means of agreements on often costly non-price restrictions that it will have the most interest in the distributors' resale prices. The manufacturer often will want to ensure that its distributors earn sufficient profit to pay for programmes such as hiring and training additional salesmen or demonstrating the technical features of the product, and will want to see that 'free-riders' do not interfere."[17]

In *Sharp Electronics*, defendant Sharp had provided suggested resale prices for its products, prices which the plaintiff's only local competitor, Hartwell, evidently largely followed. The plaintiff, however, ran a discount operation. The competitor complained to Sharp and the two agreed that plaintiff would be terminated for its discounting. The terminated discounter won a judgement at trial which was overturned by the court of appeals. The Supreme Court affirmed the appeals court's decision, finding that a per se unlawful conspiracy to maintain resale prices had not been shown as Hartwell and Sharp had not agreed on what prices to charge, even though they had agreed to terminate Business Electronics for discounting. Because the case thus fell outside the area of per se prohibition, Business Electronics would have the burden of establishing the unreasonableness of the restraint.

While the opinion thus arguably preserves the per se rule for agreements to maintain resale prices (and offers some possible anticompetitive consequences of such agreements[18]), it clearly increases as a practical matter the ability of a manufacturer to enforce "suggested" resale prices. Further, language in the opinion suggests again, as in *Spray Rite* above, that the court sees little practical difference between vertical price and non-price restraints:

> "All vertical restraints have the potential to allow dealers to increase 'prices' and can be characterized as intended to achieve just that. In fact, vertical non-price restraints only accomplish the benefits identified in *GTE Sylvania* because they reduce intrabrand price competition to the point where the dealer's profit margin permits provision of the desired services. As we described it in Monsanto: 'the manufacturer often will want to ensure that its distributors earn sufficient profit to pay for programmes such as hiring and training additional salesmen or demonstrating the technical features of the product, and will want to see that 'free-riders' do not interfere."[19]

These decisions imply that patentees will have at least as much, if not greater, freedom to establish prices by their licensees than now exists in the distribution of non-patented goods. Thus, the earlier cases presented above, such as *Univis*, where the Court reached to find exhaustion and then per se illegality, seem unlikely to be decided in a similar fashion today. On the other hand, cases such as *Gypsum*, where resale price maintenance by the patentee seemed plainly aimed at cartelizing an industry, would probably be decided in a similar fashion today.

EEC

In the EEC, the patent licensing block exemption[20] denies the benefits of the block exemption for any agreement where "one party is restricted in the determination of prices, components of prices or discounts for the licensed products"[21]. The know-how licensing block exemption operates in the same fashion[22].

B. OUTPUT RESTRAINTS

France

In France, a 1971 decision by the Competition Commission in the matter of *plastic cases for bottles*[23] involved proposed output restraints among case manufacturers. The matter arose when bottlers of mineral water, beer and wine sought to have developed a standardized, reusable plastic case through a corporation formed for that purpose, La Société pour le Développement du Casier à Bouteilles Standard (SD). SD conducted a design competition, the results of which were never announced, and then later accepted as its standard a model jointly submitted after the competition by two plastics firms, Allibert and Plastimonde, the latter firm holding the exclusive licence in France of a German patent necessary for the production of such cases. These firms ceded to SD their industrial design rights in the new case and SD (later supplanted by another group, CFP) limited in absolute terms the permissible production of the new cases by firms other than Allibert and Plastimonde. The agreements also forbade other case manufacturers to produce other plastic cases which could be used or confused with the registered design.

The Competition Commission found that these actions amounted to an abuse of a joint dominant position by Allibert and Plastimonde, as the supply of plastic cases was sharply restricted, especially in 1968, when only one other firm (and a small one) was granted permission by CFP to supply the cases. In 1969, however, the restraint began to ease, as CFP licensed seven other manufacturers and the appearance of plastic bottles in disposable packaging produced in a short time excess capacity in plastic case manufacturing. Nonetheless, CFP was continuing to restrain production and the Commission found an abuse of a dominant position in violation of Article 59 bis of the Ordonnance of 30th June 1945. This violation, moreover, was not excused as favouring economic progress under Article 59 ter as the economic benefits of the new standardized case were due to the efforts at standardization generally rather than to the particular acts of Allibert and Plastimonde.

Japan

In its decision in *Nippon Concrete Industries Co. and Five Others* in 1970, the FTC showed that the respondent companies could not be allowed to collectively fix the market shares of each company nor oblige the third party licensees to observe the market sharing agreement determined by the licensors-respondents. The six manufacturer-suppliers of pre-stressed concrete piles (PC piles), who each owned important patent and utility model rights for the piles and exchanged these rights with one another, concluded agreements on market sharing and licensing conditions. Licensing of any one company was allowed only when the other five companies agreed and also when the licensee undertook to adhere to the market-sharing agreement. The FTC found that these agreements violated Section 3 (prohibition of unreasonable restraint of trade) since through these restrictions the competition in the PC pile market was substantially restricted. The FTC ordered the six companies to eliminate the agreements.

The new FTC Guidelines provide that patent or know-how licensing agreements which set minimum domestic output on the licensee would not be considered to be unfair. Agreements setting maximum or minimum export quantities would likewise not be unfair, provided that the export market met one of the three conditions identified earlier (where a patent was registered, the licensor was routinely marketing or a third party was granted exclusive rights). If none of the three conditions applied, the limitation on export quantities might be found to be unfair after case-by-case analysis. Maximum output restriction of the licensee in the domestic market is not specifically discussed, but could be condemned to be unfair in such cases where output restriction is used as a means to affect cartel agreements or private monopolization.

Sweden

In the *Dubbman* case, discussed in Part A above, the challenged agreement included quota provisions as well as price restraints. While the Market Court found that price clauses were outside the scope of patent protection, it found that the output restraints probably were within the framework of the patent grant. Nonetheless, the Court struck down the output restraints along with the price restraints due to the impact on price formation, efficiency and the trade of third parties. In reaching this result the Court essentially balanced the harmful effects of the restraint against the rights of the patentee and found the harmful effects to be excessive in this particular case.

United States

A pure output restraint unaccompanied by price provisions arose in *Q-Tips Inc. v. Johnson and Johnson*[24], where Q-Tips licensed Johnson and Johnson to use its patented cotton-swab making machine, but limited the number of unpatented swabs which Johnson and Johnson could make. When Johnson and Johnson violated the agreement, Q-Tips sued for infringement. Johnson and Johnson argued that the quantity limitation was misuse of the patent, thus Q-Tips should be estopped from enforcing its patent. The district court, however, disagreed, and found the quantity limitation not to bar an action for infringement, noting that under the patent the plaintiff could bar any use at all of its patented machine. The court's opinion gave considerable weight to the fact that Q-Tips did not try to impose price restraints as well, and thus distinguished such cases as *United States Gypsum* and *Line Materials* discussed in Part A above.

EEC

The patent and know-how block exemptions give similar but not identical treatment to output restraints. Under the patent licensing regulation, a quantity restraint results in the licensing agreement losing the benefit of the block exemption[25]. The know-how exemption provides similarly but also provides that an output limiting agreement may be exempted where it is designed *(a)* to limit the licensee to supply its own needs, *(b)* to prohibit the licensee from constructing facilities for third parties or *(c)* to provide a particular customer with a second source of supply[26].

Even though output limiting licenses do not benefit from either block exemption and normally would be prohibited under Article 85(1), they may nonetheless be exempted under Article 85(3). One case where that issue arose is *ENI/Montedison*, involving cross-licensing of patents and know-how in the chemicals and thermoplastics industries[27]. The agreements between ENI, an Italian state holding company, and Montedison, a private Italian chemicals and pharmaceuticals firm, related to their efforts to rationalize their production in certain chemical feedstocks and in thermoplastics, industries suffering from serious over-capacity in the EC. The firms agreed to reduce their cracking capacities at the feedstock level and to specialize at the thermoplastic level, with each firm ceasing the production of certain thermoplastics. Patents and know-how were cross-licensed on a non-exclusive basis in connection with the plan.

The Commission exempted the agreements under Article 85(3) as they helped to resolve a serious problem of overcapacity more quickly and completely than would have otherwise been possible. Moreover, the fact that each firm retained cracking capacity and the right to use its own intellectual property (the patents and know-how were licensed non-exclusively, not assigned), meant that each firm remained a potential competitor in the thermoplastics lines it had abandoned, limiting the restraint on competition.

C. TERRITORIAL RESTRAINTS

Japan

In the *Yakult* case, described in Part A above, involving the sale of a fermented milk product by local bottlers, the Fair Trade Commission found a violation of Section 19 of the Antimonopoly Act in part due to the imposition of territorial restraints upon local retailers of the beverage.

Restrictions on export territories in patent or know-how licensing agreements may also violate the Antimonopoly Act under the FTC's Guidelines. Restrictions on territories to which the licensee may export may be found to be unfair after case-by-case analysis unless the territory is one in which the licensor already does business, has already granted an exclusive licence to another party, or has patent rights. Also, territorial restrictions within Japan which are covered by the patent rights are not considered to be unfair, as they are within the proper exercise of rights under the Patent Act.

Sweden

The ability of a Swedish patentee to impose territorial restraints within the Swedish market is limited by the exhaustion principle; once a patented item is manufactured and sold in Sweden the buyer may use it as he sees fit, free of territorial or other restraints. Territorial restraints may arise, however, in the international context and an enterprise which holds the Swedish patent has the right to prevent parallel importation of the product into Sweden. Swedish patentees may control both the export and import of patented goods. In one case, however, NO intervened against a patentee seeking to extend these restraints to non-licensed products[28]. An example of a permissible international territorial restraint can be seen in NO's handling of a matter involving imports of *fibreglass products* from Norway. The Swedish patentee sought to block these imports as infringing the patent, even though they were manufactured by the Norwegian licensee. Given the infringement of the Swedish patent and the absence of special circumstances, NO declined to proceed against the Swedish patentee[29]. On the other hand, NO did intervene in a matter involving patented *bolt gun cartridges*, where the sole Swedish licensee and the foreign holder of the Swedish patent acted to block parallel imports. When the patentee successfully blocked the parallel importation by a court order, the firms which had been importing the infringing cartridges sought NO's assistance in obtaining supplies from the Swedish licensee. NO instead prevailed upon the patentee and licensee to permit the resumption of parallel imports in an effort to lower the price of these cartridges[30].

United States

In the United States, territorial restrictions in patent licences have long been considered permissible under the Patent Act, which permits licenses for "any specified part of the United States"[31]. What becomes relevant, then, is what restrictions the patentee may impose once his patent rights are exhausted by the first authorized sale. At that point, the patentee's ability to impose territorial restraints would be like that of a know-how licensor or the manufacturer of any non-patented product. The antitrust consequences of such *vertical* territorial restraints have changed considerably in the United States in recent years under the Supreme Court's decision in *GTE-Sylvania*, where the Court noted the many procompetitive aspects of vertical restraints generally and thus found per se illegality of vertical territorial restraints to be unwarranted. According to the Court:

"Vertical restrictions promote interbrand competition by allowing the manufacturer to achieve certain efficiencies in the distribution of his products. Economists have identified a number of ways in which manufacturers can use such restrictions to compete more effectively against other manufacturers. For example, new manufacturers and manufacturers entering new markets can use the restrictions in order to induce competent and aggressive retailers to make the kind of investment of capital and labour that is often required in the distribution of products unknown to the consumer. Established manufacturers can use them to induce retailers to engage in promotional activities or to provide service and repair facilities necessary to the efficient marketing of their products. Service and repair are vital for many products, such as automobiles and major household appliances. The availability and quality of such services affect a manufacturer's goodwill and the competitiveness of his product. Because of market imperfections such as the so-called "free rider" effect, these services might not be provided by retailers in a purely competitive situation, despite the fact that each retailer's benefit would be greater if all provided the services than if none did."[32]

The Court recognized that vertical territorial restraints could limit intrabrand competition but found that the ability of the retailer to exploit the local market was limited both by the mobility of consumers and the presence of interbrand competition[33]. Further, the Court, citing Bork and Posner, gave credence to the argument that a manufacturer has an interest in maintaining as much intrabrand competition as is consistent with the efficient distribution of its products[34].

The decision in *GTE-Sylvania*, by focusing on the importance of interbrand rather than intrabrand competition and accepting the procompetitive effects of vertical territorial restraints, marked a turning point in the Court's treatment of vertical restraints generally, substantially narrowing the areas subject to a rule of per se illegality. Indeed, the recent opinion in *Sharp Electronics* discussed in Part A above shows how the reasoning of the decision is now being applied to the area of resale price maintenance.

The rules applicable to territorial restraints in international patent and know-how licensing follow directly from the rules applied domestically. In *Dunlop Co. v. Kelsey-Hayes Co.*[35], involving an action by the UK firm Dunlop as the holder of certain disk-brake patents to enjoin infringements by its former American sub-licensee Kelsey-Hayes, the court of appeals affirmed the district court finding that no infringement had occurred and then turned to Kelsey-Hayes' cross appeal on an antitrust counterclaim, which sought treble damages for Dunlop's alleged horizontal division of world markets through its patent licensing. Kelsey-Hayes alleged that this was accomplished by Dunlop's restraining licensees in Japan, Italy, Germany and Australia from exporting to the United States. The court of appeals disagreed, however, finding that Dunlop was merely creating territorial licences on an international scale in the same fashion as a patentee could do within the United States under the Patent Act. Thus, no antitrust violation was found.

A territorial restraint similar in effect to that of the *Dunlop* case can be created if a holder of American patents licenses a foreign firm only under parallel foreign patents, leaving the foreign firm subject to an infringement action if it sought to export to the United States. These facts arose in *United States v. Westinghouse Electric Corp.*[36], where the government challenged Westinghouse's refusal to grant licences under its US patents to Mitsubishi, its Japanese licensee. The Court found this refusal to be no more than a tactic "normally and reasonably adapted to secure pecuniary reward for the patent monopoly", relying on the *General Electric* decision discussed in Part A above[37]. Further, the government's theory could not be reconciled with the rule that holders of United States patents may refuse to license them[38]. Thus the international territorial division created by Westinghouse did not amount to a violation of Section 1 of the Sherman Act.

The DOJ Guidelines describes the DOJ's enforcement policy with respect to both international and domestic territorial restraints generally and in the context of a hypothetical transnational know-how licensing arrangement. (The Guidelines state that the same analysis applies to patent licensing.) In the Guidelines hypothetical, a US firm licenses unpatented know-how that it uses to produce product X to two foreign firms, one of which sells X in the United States[39]. The foreign licensees are prohibited by the licences from selling X in the United States, whether the X is manufactured using the licensed technology or not. Each foreign licensee is granted an exclusive territory outside the United States in which to sell X. The DOJ Guidelines note that because the division of foreign markets lacks a direct effect on US commerce, it is not subject to the jurisdiction of the US antitrust laws. However, the agreement of the foreign licensees not to sell X in the United States is subject to the jurisdiction of the US antitrust laws. The DOJ's analysis of those agreements in each case turns on whether the foreign licensee does or would compete in the sale of X in the United States if not for the licence restriction. If the licence does eliminate competition then, using the DOJ's normal merger standards, the DOJ determines whether the complete integration of price and output decisions through merger between the US licensor and its foreign licensee(s) would be anticompetitive. If a merger would be anticompetitive, then the DOJ considers unique efficiencies that would result from the licensing arrangement and whether the licence is less restrictive than an outright merger to determine whether, on balance, the licence is anticompetitive[40].

EEC

Territorial restraints have received considerable attention in the EEC, reflecting the overriding goal of market integration. Thus territorial restrictions in all types of intellectual property licensing agreements have been the subject of decisions by the Commission and the Court of Justice, and such restrictions receive extensive treatment in the two block exemptions. Territorial restrictions on the licensee often go hand-in-hand with a grant of exclusivity by the licensor for that territory. Issues concerning exclusivity, however, are reserved for Part D below.

The Commission's policy towards territorial restrictions is aimed at preserving the free movement of goods within the Community balanced against the need to give firms sufficient incentives to invest in a given teritory. The Commission's policy on free movement follows from Articles 30 and 34 of Treaty of Rome as well as Court of Justice decisions which establish an exhaustion doctrine in the Community.

That doctrine was set out for patented goods in *Centrafarm BV v. Sterling Drug Inc.*, which involved an effort by Sterling, holder of drug patents in both the UK and the Netherlands, to block parallel imports by Centrafarm from one country to the other[41]. The Court held that while Article 36 preserved the existence of national patent rights, the exercise of those rights could be regulated. Further, the principle of free movement of goods under Article 30 required that the rights of the patentee be narrowly construed. Thus, "in relation to patents, the specific subject matter of the industrial property is the guarantee that the patentee, to reward the creative effort of the inventor, has the exclusive right to use and invention with a view to manufacturing industrial products and putting them into circulation for the first time, either directly or by the grant of licences to third parties, as well as the right to oppose infringements.

An obstacle to the free movement of goods may arise out of the existence, within a national legislation concerning industrial and commercial property, of provisions laying down that a patentee's right is not exhausted when the product protected by the patent is marketed in another Member State, with the result that the patentee can prevent importation of the product into his own Member State when it has been marketed in another State.

Whereas an obstacle to the free movement of goods of this kind may be justified on the ground of protection of industrial property where such protection is invoked against a product coming from a Member State where it is not patentable and has been manufactured by third parties without the consent of the patentee and in cases where there exist patents, the original proprietors of which are legally and economically independent, a derogation from the principle of the free movement of goods is not, however, justified where the product has been put onto the market in a legal manner, by the patentee himself or with his consent, in the Member State from which it has been imported, in particular in the case of a proprietor of parallel patents."[42]

This exhaustion doctrine, aimed at preserving parallel imports, is basic to understanding the Commission's policy towards territorial restraints in patent and know-how licensing agreements. Thus, for example, the Commission was favourably disposed to grant negative clearance to the patent and know-how licensing agreements in *Burroughs/Geha-Werke*[43] and *Burroughs/Delplanque*[44], establishing exclusive licensees in Germany and France respectively for the manufacture of a type of carbon paper, as each licensee was free to export anywhere in the Community. The Commission also granted negative clearance to a patent and know-how licensing agreement in *Raymond-Nagoya*, where the Japanese firm Nagoya was licensed to manufacture and sell small plastic pieces used in automobile manufacturing but only in Japan and neighbouring markets. The Commission granted negative clearance based on a lack of impact on trade within the Community even though Nagoya accepted a ban on exports to the EC, as the Commission found that the practical barriers to such exports were likely to be insurmountable[45]. A similar result can be found in *Kabelmetal/Luchaire*, a patent and know-how licensing agreement between the German firm Kabelmetal and the French firm Luchaire concerning technology for the forming and machining of metal parts[46]. The Commission ultimately exempted the agreement under Article 85(3) but only after a clause prohibiting exports by Luchaire to other countries within the EC was deleted. Notably, the Commission did not oppose a ban on exports outside the EC as that restraint did not affect intra-Community trade.

More recently, the issues of exclusivity and territorial restraints in the context of intellectual property licensing were reviewed by the Court of Justice in *Nungesser v. Commission* (the *Maize Seed* decision)[47]. That case arose out of a Commission challenge to agreements related to the marketing of a new hybrid maize seed. Plant breeders' rights in the seeds were held by the French research institute which had developed them, l'Institut National de la Recherche Agronomique ("INRA"), and this institute had contracted with Nungesser for the reproduction and sale of the seeds in Germany. The agreements with INRA and Nungesser provided, inter alia, that Nungesser had the exclusive licence for

Germany, that INRA or those deriving rights through INRA would not export to the German market and that INRA would seek to prevent other firms from exporting the seeds to Germany. The Commission reviewed these agreements, found them to be in violation of Article 85(1) and not to be exempted under Article 85(3).

The Court's review of the Commission's opinion is noteworthy for its delineation of how far a licence agreement may go in seeking to establish an exclusive territory for a licensee. Further, the opinion by its terms is applicable generally to intellectual property licensing even though the case involved plant breeder's rights. In this regard, the firms had argued that the special nature of the hybrid seed business, e.g. the need to take into account local climate and soil conditions, supported a degree of territorial protection otherwise not permitted under the competition rules, a view supported inter alia, by the French government, which also argued that technical innovation in the creation of plant species required the possibility of granting absolute territorial protection.

The Court, however, was not persuaded that these considerations merited special competition rules for plant breeders:

> "[T]hat line of argument fails to take into account, however, that many products capable of forming the subject-matter of a trade mark or a patent, in particular certain food or pharmaceutical products, are in a similar situation. Although the reasons put forward by the applicants are based on correct findings of fact, they are not sufficient to justify a special system for breeders' rights in relation to other industrial or commercial property rights."[48]

While breeders' rights are thus subject to the same competition rules for other intellectual property rights, the Court did add that the specific nature of the products involved could be taken into account[49].

The Court then turned to the Commission's analysis of the exclusive licence and related territorial restraints under Article 85(1). The Court broke down the question as follows: first, the grant of an exclusive licence for Germany, standing alone, created an "open exclusive licence", open in that it did not seek to block parallel imports from elsewhere in the Community. The Court reversed the Commission on this point, finding that the creation of an open exclusive licence did not amount to a restriction of competition within Article 85(1), a point developed in greater detail in Part D below. Second, the Court examined the territorial restraints added to the open exclusive licence, whereby INRA agreed not to export to Germany and to seek to prevent others from engaging in parallel importing. These efforts to create absolute territorial protection the Court found to be contrary to the Treaty as they could result in the "artificial maintenance of separate national markets"[50]. On this point the UK Government argued that there could be no restriction on intracommunity trade, and thus no agreement prohibited by Article 85(1), as the agreements could not prevent parallel importing under the exhaustion doctrine already established in the EC. Nonetheless, because the parties intended to restrict trade, the Court found the agreements to be prohibited by Article 85(1), thus affirming the Commission on this point[51].

The Court also affirmed the Commission's denial of an exemption under Article 85(3) for the provisions creating absolute territorial protection. In this regard it rejected arguments by the UK that the provisions encouraged the licensee to exploit its rights, thus increasing production and distribution and promoting technical and economic progress. The Court further rejected arguments by the French plant licensing authority that the restrictions were due to the fragile, technically advanced nature of the seeds and that the restriction in any event did not substantially eliminate competition, as numerous other varieties of maize seed were present on the market.

The Court's rejection of the last point shows how absolute territorial restraints, and probably other restraints as well, can be prohibited per se without regard to their actual impact on competition. The Court did not dispute that substitute seeds existed for the purposes of Article 85(3)(b) (whether the agreement affords "the possibility of eliminating competition in respect of a substantial part of the products in question") but found that the exemption was properly denied because it was not shown that the absolute territorial restraints were "indispensable" to promote economic progress under Article 85(3)(a)[52]. Thus, it appears that once a territorial restraint is caught by Article 85(1), it may be difficult to avoid a prohibition, as the parties bear the burden of proving the restriction to be "indispensable". Second, it emerges from *Maize Seed* that the Court is focused on *intrabrand* competition; the original finding that the agreements restricted competition deals with the effects on competition in this particular hybrid seed, without regard to the existence of effective competition from other maize seeds.

The Commission's patent licensing block exemption was published two years after the Court's decision in *Maize Seed*, and follows the basic distinction in that decision between "open" and "absolute" territorial restraints, with provisions related to open territorial restraints tending to be exempted under Article 1 and provisions related to absolute territorial protection falling in the so-called "black list" of Article 3. In particular, Article 1 exempts agreements where the licensor binds himself not to sell in the territory or to license others there[53], the licensee agrees not to "exploit" the licence in territories reserved for the licensor (for the duration of the patent)[54] or to "manufacture or use" the patented product or process in territories licensed to others[55]. Further, the regulation draws a distinction between active and passive sales and exempts agreements which prohibit the licensee from engaging in "an active policy of putting the licensed product on the market" in territories licensed to others[56]. Further, the licensee may be bound not to put the product on the market at all in other territories for up to five years from the introduction of the product in the Common Market[57]. However, a clause prohibiting passive sales for more than five years takes the agreement out of the block exemption[58]. The same result follows if either party is obliged not to sell to parallel importers or to make it difficult for such importers to obtain supplies[59].

Following the publication of the patent licensing regulation but before the appearance of the know-how regulation, the Commission considered a licensing agreement involving predominantly know-how between two manufacturers of coated flat glass. In that decision, *Boussois/Interpane*, the German firm Interpane undertook to provide its technology for coating flat glass, one of several currently in use, to the French firm Boussois[60]. Under the agreement Boussois received the exclusive right to sell in France for five years and a non-exclusive right thereafter, as well as outside France on a non-exclusive basis indefinitely. Boussois was not licensed, however, to manufacture outside France, limiting the ability of Boussois to sell there as a practical matter because the product is difficult and costly to transport.

The Commission's opinion found that these restrictions as well as others brought the agreement within the scope of Article 85(1). Further, the patent-licensing block exemption was inapplicable, as the agreement involved predominantly know-how and parallel patents did not exist in five Member States. Thus the Commission considered whether the conditions of Article 85(3) were met.

The Commission's treatment of the exemption question shows movement from its earlier decisions and from the Court's opinion in *Maize Seed*. Notable is the finding that the agreement will not eliminate competition as there is effective interbrand competition within the Community. In this regard the Commission noted that the agreement did not prevent parallel importing, which it termed "quite possible" despite the transportation barriers described above. Further, and also unlike *Maize Seed*, the Commission readily found that the restrictions were indispensable to the success of the agreement.

The favourable reception which the Commission gave the *Boussois* know-how agreement presaged the know-how block exemption, a draft of which was issued the following year. That exemption follows the pattern for territorial restrictions which the Commission adopted in its patent licensing exemption set out above but sets specific time limits for certain provisions. In particular, the regulation provides for a ten-year limit on the exemption granted for territorial restrictions, reduced to five years (as in the case of the patent regulation) for restrictions on passive sales to other territories[61].

D. EXCLUSIVITY

Two aspects of efforts by licensors and licensees to establish exclusive relationships are discussed here. One type of relationship included in this part is where the licensor agrees not to create a second licensee in the territory. These cases thus follow from and are closely related to the cases involving territorial restraints discussed in the Part C above. A second type of exclusivity presented here relates to commitments by the licensee to deal exclusively with the licensor.

Australia

In *Transfield Pty. Ltd. v. Arlo International Ltd.*[62], the Australian High Court dealt, albeit obliquely, with the issue of exclusive dealing in a patent licensing context. In that case, Arlo had granted Transfield the exclusive licence in Australia for its patented telescoping utility poles. A clause in the licensing agreement committed Transfield to use its "best efforts" to promote the pole in Australia. When Transfield encountered problems in erecting the poles, however, it simply abandoned that design and began selling a similar pole of its own design. At trial, Arlo obtained a judgement for nearly A$300 000 which was upheld by the Court of Appeal. The High Court likewise affirmed the verdict even though Section 112 of the Patents Act 1952 prohibits most kinds of exclusive dealing clauses in licensing agreements. (Only exclusive sales clauses are permitted; here Transfield was "using", not selling, the Arlo process.) A majority of Justices sidestepped the Patents Act issue by finding that the clause did not literally prohibit Transfield from dealing with others but merely required it to use its best efforts in promoting Arlo's design, which it had not done by dropping the design when difficulties arose rather than trying to overcome them. The opinions of the majority further found that the best-efforts clause was not unenforceable under Section 45 of the Trade Practices Act 1974 as a clause with the purpose or likely effect of substantially lessening competition. Rather, the justices found that the best-efforts clause promoted rather than restrained competition and, in any event, was exempted from Section 45 by Section 51(3)(a) of the Trade Practices Act as a clause authorised under the Patents Act.

Denmark

In 1962 the MCA considered whether a patent licensing agreement in which the licensor agreed to license only members of a certain trade association caused an adverse effect as described in the Monopolies Act. The holder of a Danish patent for the production of a *permanent fluid*[63] drew up a standard licensing agreement in co-operation with the Association of Suppliers to the Hairdresser Trade (ASH) which limited the patent holder to enter licensing agreements with firms which were members of the ASH. A factory which produced and sold perfume, toiletries and commodities to hairdressers and which was already a member of the Trade Organisation of Perfumery and Toilet Commodities complained to the MCA. The firm argued that it was unreasonable to be forced to become a member of the ASH and pay entrance fee and membership fees. The MCA considered it reasonable if a patent licensing agreement listed terms ensuring that a licensee had "a natural connection to the line of trade and the qualifications to utilize the patent soundly, since (the patent holder) had a justified interest in ensuring that the permanent fluid kept a certain standard, even if the commodity was marketed in the name of the licensee and not in the name or under the trade mark of the patent holder". If a potential licensee otherwise fulfilled the listed conditions, however, the MCA stated that it would consider terms limiting the utilisation of the patent to members of a particular trade organisation as "unreasonable market conditions in contravention of the Monopolies Act, Section 11, Subsection 1". The case was resolved through a negotiated settlement between the involved parties, under which the patent holder entered into a patent licensing agreement with the potential licensee without the latter becoming a member of ASH, but on the condition that the licensee fulfilled certain financial qualifications.

France

The Competition Commission issued an opinion in 1962 concerning an agreement among *stretch yarn manufacturers*[64] due to their efforts to maintain exclusive dealing relationships with their customers. In that matter, the Swiss holder of patents for the manufacturer of "Helanca" nylon stretch yarns, a single French licensee and a number of French sub-licensees organised themselves into a professional union called the "Syndicat de Défense et de Promotion Helanca - France" and sought to limit output and fix prices of nylon stretch yarn in France. Apparently, the patents concerned a machine providing the only economic method for spinning certain nylon stretch yarns available at the time and the Swiss patentee permitted only members of the cartel to import the patented spinning machines.

One technique used by the syndicate from mid-1953 until the beginning of 1962, approximately when the cartel ceased to function effectively, was a system of loyalty rebates aimed at maintaining exclusivity with their customers. The Competition Commission found that Article 59 bis of the Ordinance of 30th June 1945 applicable to these rebate practices in spite of the syndicate's argument that the agreement to issue rebates did not involve an agreement prohibited under Article 59 bis if the agreement was among a patentee and his licencee and sub-licensees. The Commission disagreed, however, finding that the agreement was not exempt just because patents were involved, given that it operated to limit competition among the parties. Further, even though the Commission recognised that the syndicate helped the "remarkable" development of the stretch yarn industry in France, it

66

could not exempt the restrictive practices from Article 59 bis because the restrictions were not shown to be necessary to the achievement of those benefits.

Germany

In a series of decisions the Federal Court had to assess the validity of non competition clauses relating to licensing agreements.

The first decision *Schweissbolzen* handed down in 1966 concerned a "sub-licensing agreement" by which the holder of an exclusive licence for welding equipment concluded an exclusive purchasing arrangement with the defendant who was to fabricate the licensed products[65]. On his part the defendant undertook not to produce or sell during the duration of the contract any goods produced under a competing technology or otherwise similar to the patented product. Subsequently, the parties disagreed on the validity of the clause and the plaintiff resorted successfully to arbitration. The Court set aside the arbitral award as contrary to the ARC.

The first question to be resolved was whether a contract of this type could be considered a licensing agreement to which Section 20 of the ARC would apply. This was denied by several authors who argued that Section 20 was an exception to the more general provisions of the Act concerning horizontal or vertical restraints which should be narrowly construed and therefore not applied to mixed contracts involving the use of licensed patents by a third party. The Court rejected these arguments, considering that the use of a licence and the types of restraints imposed by the contract were the decisive feature of the case justifying the application of Section 20. The underlying rationale of this section which was to prevent the misuse of the exclusive right conferred by a patent through restraints going beyond the scope of the protected right.

The Court then considered whether the contested clause was covered by Section 20, subsection 2, 1 exempting restrictions imposed on the acquirer or licensee insofar as they are justified by the seller's or licensor's interest in a technically satisfactory exploitation of the protected matter. In the view of the Court this was not the case as the defendant had always satisfactorily complied with his obligation to supply the plaintiff with the products fabricated under licence. Therefore the restriction imposed on the defendant not to produce or sell any competing or similar products was considered unreasonable as it exceeded the scope of the protected right.

Another case decided in 1967, *Fischverarbeitungs-maschine*[66] involved the enforceability of a non-competition clause after the termination of a licensing agreement. The plaintiff, inventor of a fish processing machine, filed for patent protection in several countries, including Germany. While his application was refused by the German Federal Patent Office, the patents were granted elsewhere. Subsequent to the refusal of the patent in Germany, he concluded with the defendant a licensing agreement granting him a worldwide license for the production and the sale of the machine. The contract was terminated by the licensor after two years and in the following litigation the licensee agreed to an out-of-court settlement in which he undertook to abstain from future production or sale of the machine. On the basis of this agreement the plaintiff filed suit alleging that the defendant had subsequently produced and sold a number of machines in Germany.

The Federal Court first considered the applicability of the German ARC given the fact that the contract related to the use of a foreign patent by a German licensee. It concluded that section 20 was applicable as the restraints on competition attached to the licensing agreement produced effects within the German territory. The Court then found the restriction to be unreasonable and exceeding the scope or the protected right to the extent that they applied to a territory (i.e. Germany) where patent protection had been refused.

A third case, *Fertigbeton*, decided in 1976, concerned a vertical relationship between the parties with horizontal market sharing elements[67]. Although the contract did not involve a patent or another intellectual property right, the Court's holding concerning the exclusivity features of the contract would seem to apply to IPR licensing arrangements having similar features.

The defendant a producer of concrete, had committed himself to purchase raw material exclusively from the plaintiff, who undertook not to produce or sell concrete within the territory of the defendant. The Court considered this latter undertaking to be a horizontal constraint which was invalid according to Section 1 of the ARC. Although the contractual relationship between the parties was vertical in nature the restriction on the plaintiff not to compete in the defendant's territory excluded him as a potential supplier to this part of the market. This feature of the arrangement, in the view of the Court, also pursued a common purpose between the parties in the sense of Section 1, i.e. market sharing in restraint of competition.

A subsequent case *Frischbeton*, decided in 1979, had similar but also some distinctive features[68]. The defendant had established a number of companies engaged in the production of concrete within a given territory. Following a liquidity crisis he transferred his shares to a competitor who agreed also to take over all existing debts. In exchange, the defendant undertook not to establish during a period of ten years any competing new companies within the competitor's territory nor to acquire any participation in such a company. In the following litigation the Court examined the validity of this clause under the ARC. Despite the horizontal character of the restraint it concluded that there was no violation of Section 1 because the parties did not pursue a common purpose, i.e. the contract did not serve a common interest of both parties but exclusively the plaintiff's interest to eliminate the defendant as an actual or potential competitor within a segment of the market. Nevertheless, the contract was held null and void under Section 138 of the Civil Code as the duration of the non-competition clause was out of proportion with the plaintiff's reasonable interest unduly restricted the defendant in his future commercial activities and therefore acted contra bonos mores.

Japan

The *Yakult* fermented milk case described in Part A above included an aspect of exclusive dealing. The patent and trademark licensing agreements between Yakult and its bottlers required its bottlers to sell only to retailers who, inter alia, agreed not to sell competing products. The FTC ordered Yakult to delete the clause as it was not recognized as an exercise of patent and trademark rights.

The FTC's Guidelines for patent and know-how licensing agreements give considerable attention to issues related to exclusivity. For patent licensing agreements, restrictions against handling competing goods or using competing technology after the expiration of the licensing agreement would be highly likely to be considered to be unfair. Such restrictions during the term of the agreement may be considered to be unfair. "Best efforts" requirements falling short of exclusivity will not be considered to be unfair. The Guidelines also cover restrictions on research and development activities by the licensee, finding that restrictions on licensee research into either the licensed or other technology highly likely to be unfair. Know-how licensing agreements are treated similarly to the patent agreements discussed above but there are certain differences reflecting the need to maintain secrecy and the difficulty in policing unauthorized use. In particular, a know-how licensor will be able to prohibit the licensee from using competing technology or from handling competing goods for a "short period" following the termination of the licensing agreement "insofar as it is difficult to prevent unauthorized exploitation of the licensed know-how by such restrictions as a use ban after the expiration or termination of the agreement". That is, such restrictions will not be considered to be unfair. If the unauthorized exploitation consideration were absent, however, such a restriction would, as in the case of patents, be considered to be "highly likely" to be unfair.

Sweden

An exclusive licence in Sweden for the manufacture of *fibre glass* was reviewed by NO, which considered ordering the French patentee to grant additional licences. While NO found that real competition in fibre glass manufactured by that technique could occur only if additional licences were granted, it did not consider the situation sufficiently compelling under *Dubbman* to set aside the patentee's rights as other usable methods of manufacturing the product existed[69].

United States

In the United States there is no legal barrier under the antitrust laws for a patentee to grant an exclusive licence; the Patent Act specifically provides that licences may be exclusive[70]. An agreement providing for the transfer of know-how would not, however, benefit from that provision and thus could in theory be subject to action under the antitrust laws. As a non-price vertical restraint, such an agreement would be subject to a rule of reason analysis under the doctrine of *GTE Sylvania* discussed above.

Efforts by the patent licensor to obtain a commitment of exclusivity by the licensee are not provided for under the Patent Act and thus are subject both to potential attack under the Sherman and Clayton Acts and to a defence of patent misuse by an infringer. An example of the latter situation can be seen in *National Lockwasher Co. v. George K. Garrett Co.*[71] where the patentee of a type of lockwasher included in several standard-form contracts with manufacturing licensees that the licensee not produce competing lockwashers. When the patentee sought to enforce the patent against an infringer, it found its patent unenforceable due to the "misuse" of requiring exclusivity by its licensees.

The decision in *National Lockwasher* is illustrative of how conclusory analysis can become under the doctrine of patent misuse. The court of appeals analogised from tie-in cases involving a patented article and found the patentee's practices here to similarly involve the use of "the lawful monopoly granted by the patent as a means of suppressing the manufacture and sale of competing unpatented articles"[72]. The opinion, however, is devoid of any discussion of how that suppression of competition would arise; the fact that the product was patented was sufficient to short-circuit any analysis.

The type of analysis which would be applied to a know-how agreement (or to patent licensing agreements if the presumption of market power should be eliminated) was recently set forth in *Jefferson Parish Hospital Dist. No. 2 v. Hyde*[73], a case variously characterised as involving either a tie-in or exclusive dealing arrangement and discussed in greater detail in Part G below. The dissent by four justices in that case (the majority treated the contract as a tie-in) set forth a succinct analysis of exclusive dealing under the rule of reason:

"Exclusive-dealing arrangements may, in some circumstances, create or extend market power of a supplier or the purchaser party to the exclusive-dealing arrangement, and may thus restrain horizontal competition. Exclusive dealing can have adverse economic consequences by allowing one supplier of goods or services unreasonably to deprive other suppliers of a market for their goods, or by allowing one buyer of goods unreasonably to deprive other buyers of a needed source of supply. In determining whether an exclusive-dealing contract is unreasonable, the proper focus is on the structure of the market for the products or services in question — the number of sellers and buyers in the market, the volume of their business, and the ease with which buyers and sellers can redirect their purchases or sales to others. Exclusive dealing is an unreasonable restraint on trade only when a significant fraction of buyers or sellers are frozen out of a market by the exclusive deal. When the sellers of services are numerous and mobile, and the number of buyers is large, exclusive-dealing arrangements of narrow scope pose no threat of adverse economic consequences. To the contrary, they may be substantially procompetive by ensuring stable markets and encouraging long-term, mutually advantageous business relationships."[74]

Finally, the DOJ's Guidelines illustrate its analysis of exclusive licensing provisions in two hypotheticals. In Case 10, a US firm grants to a US firm and a foreign firm exclusive field-of-use licences covering patented coating material. The licence allows the foreign licensee to make and sell outside the US safety eyeglasses coated with the licensed material; the foreign licensee is denied a licence to make and sell coated safety eyeglasses in the United States in competition with the US licensee. After concluding that the licences involve the legitimate transfer of valuable technology and are not sham, the DOJ Guidelines apply a rule of reason analysis. The DOJ concludes that because neither the US nor the foreign licensee do (or would) compete with the licensor in the sale of technology or safety eyeglasses, the licence does not unreasonably restrain competition between the licensor and its licensees. The DOJ Guidelines also conclude that the licence would not be anticompetitive by facilitating collusion between the US and the foreign licensees bacause, on the facts of the case, the relevant market for safety eyeglasses is not concentrated and entry is not difficult. The licensor is not required to create competition in its technology among its licensees. The DOJ Guidelines describe the potential procompetitive effects of the exclusive licence, which the DOJ would consider if it appeared that the licence would be anticompetitive. According to the DOJ Guidelines:

"The principal value of a patent is the right to its exclusive use. A licensor may properly seek to transfer this right to another person in the form of an exclusive licence to practice the patent generally, or for a specific purpose. Licensing the patent in this way may maximize the return on the patentee's investment in innovation. The grant of an exclusive licence also may encourage more efficient development and promotion of the patent by the licensee by removing the risk that other licensees, or even the patentee will benefit from those investments. It may encourage the licensee to develop innovations which, although they may not be patentable, would nevertheless make the technology more valuable to consumers. While this case involves an exclusive field-of-use licence, other forms of exclusive licences - for example, granting the licensee the exclusive rights to sell the patented product in some area of the United States or to some class of customers - can provide similar benefits."[75]

An agreement to use licensed technology exclusively can be procompetitive by giving the licensee "a strong incentive to develop and aggressively market" the licensed technology[76].

In Case 11, the DOJ Guidelines analyse an exclusive cross-licence between a US and foreign firm under which each firm obtains the right to the exclusive use of the other's technology in the licensee's own domestic market. The restriction prohibiting the foreign firm from using its competing technology in the US market is analysed as though the US firm had acquired the foreign firm's competing technology. If such an acquisition would not be challenged by the DOJ, then neither would the licence arrangement. This analysis, as summarized in the preceding chapter[77], involves a qualitative assessement of the importance of the competing technologies and, if the licence effectively eliminates competition between the licensor and licensee in the sale of a product produced using those technologies, an assessment of the structure and performance of the relevant product market or markets[78]. If the acquisition of the exclusive right would likely create, enhance, or facilitate the exercise of market power beyond that conveyed by the intellectual property itself, then the DOJ considers whether the threat of anticompetitive harm is outweighed by procompetitive efficiency benefits that the parties claim would result from the licence arrangements[79].

EEC

In the EEC exclusive licensing contracts have long been found to restrict intracommunity trade in violation of Article 85(1), although that position has been modified somewhat by the Court of Justice's opinion in *Maize Seed*.

In a number of decisions in the 1970s the Commission found exclusive licences to restrain trade in two ways. First, the licensor was restrained from competing with the licensee. Second, the licensor could not create additional licensees in the exclusive territory, eliminating potential competition between the licensee and hypothetical other licensees[80]. Because the exclusivity clause was thus typically found to be within Article 85(1), the Commission would then examine the facts to determine whether an Article 85(3) exemption could be granted. This exemption has frequently been granted following a finding that the clause was "indispensable" to induce the licensee to invest in the technology and to promote it[81].

In the *Maize Seed* case, the Commission's finding that exclusivity fell within the prohibition of Article 85(1) was sharply criticised by a number of parties and intervenors before the Court of Justice. The appellants argued that basing a violation on the exclusive nature of the agreement ignored the fact that exclusivity was necessary to introduce the new seeds and thereby to promote competition between those and other seeds. The appellants were supported in this by the British and German Governments and the French plant licensing authorities. These intervenors argued that it was incorrect to assume that every exclusive licence restricted trade in violation of Article 85(1), leaving it for the Commission to decide if the conditions of 85(3) were met.

The Court's opinion agreed with these views, at least on the facts before it. In particular, the Court drew a distinction between the grant of exclusivity in a particular territory and further steps to create "absolute" territorial exclusivity by impeding parallel imports. The Court found the former case, an "open exclusive licence" under which the licensor agrees not to grant further licences and not to compete in the territory himself, not to be within Article 85(1) at all[82].

Accordingly the Commission's subsequent patent licensing block exemption states that such "open exclusive licences" are not in themselves incompatible with Article 85(1) where they are concerned with the introduction and protection of a new technology in the licensed territory. Where in other cases agreement of this kind fall within the scope of Article 85(1) they are exempted under Article 85(3)[83].

Article 3 of the block exemption excludes from the exemption any agreements which go beyond the restrictions of Article 1 in restricting a party from competing with any other entity in the Common Market. The only exception from this "black list" prohibition is a clause requiring "best endeavours" in exploiting the licensed invention[84].

The *Interpane/Boussois* decision[85] included a treatment of an exclusivity provision in the context of know-how licensing. The exclusivity provisions, preventing other licensees from manufacturing in France and from selling there "actively or passively" for five years and preventing the licensor from manufacturing there for two years, were seen as restrictions on competition falling within the prohibitions of Article 85(1). In doing so, the Commission distinguished the agreement from the "open exclusive licences" found not to fall within Article 85(1) by the Court of Justice in *Maize Seed* based on the agreement to restrict exports to France by potential other licensees in other countries. The Commission went further, however, and did not follow *Maize Seed* with respect to the exclusivity granted to Boussois to manufacture in France. Although this could constitute an "open exclusive licence" under *Maize Seed*, the Commission found it to be a restriction on competition within Article 85(1) because it "thus restricts potential or actual competition in France during these periods from other potential French licensees and from the licensor"[86]. Thus the Commission continued to apply the same analysis of exclusivity provisions which it had developed in its decisions in the 1970s. The agreement in *Interpane/Boussois* was, however, ultimately exempted under 85(3) in part because the exclusivity provisions made Boussois more willing to invest in a plant utilising the new technology.

The know-how licensing block exemption, published following the *Interpane* decision, follows the exclusivity provisions set out in the patent licensing block exemption summarised above. In particular, obligations on the licensor or the licensee to respect exclusive territories are exempted for up to ten years, except that obligations against passive sales into other licensees' territories are exempted for only five years[87]. However, the licensing agreement loses the benefit of the block exemption if the period of exclusivity in a licensed territory exceeds the ten year limit[88]. Further, while best endeavours clauses are permitted, an exclusivity provision prohibiting either party from competing through R & D or through other products will remove the agreement from the block exemption[89]. However, where the licensee begins to compete in this fashion, the licensor may stop communicating improvements, license others and demand proof that its know-how is not being used in the competing products[90].

E.   FIELD OF USE RESTRICTIONS

Canada

In Canada, an unreported 1972 decision in *R. v. Union Carbide Ltd., et al.* involved the licensing of process and machinery patents held by Union Carbide relating to the treatment of polyethylene film for printing. A number of licensing provisions in regard to these patents were alleged to constitue abuses under Section 29, restrictions on the type of film that licensees were allowed to treat with the patented process. The case was resolved through a negotiated settlement under which the defendants agreed to revise the relevant licences to eliminate the field-of-use restrictions and other alleged anti-competitive provisions.

France

In France, a 1955 decision by the Competition Commission in the *magnesium industry*[91] examined agreements created between the Société Générale du Magnésium (a research and development and distribution organisation jointly owned by the two French magnesium manufacturers) and the six foundries which it supplied with the metal. Two of these foundries were owned by the parent firms of the Société Générale while the rest were independent. The Commission's opinion focused on restrictions imposed in Société Générale's licensing agreements with the independent foundries, especially those of Renault and SNECMA, the aircraft engine manufacturer, which limited them to using the magnesium for their internal consumption; sales to others were forbidden except in certain limited circumstances.

SNECMA in particular complained that it was thus prevented from making certain defence sales and that the resulting under-utilisation of its foundries raised its costs. SNECMA's complaint was supported by the Secretary of the French Air Force, which had to deal with a foundry related to Société Générale.

The Commission's opinion noted that the agreements created by Société général did provide some benefits in the establishment and maintenance of a fragile industry and in rationalising production. Further, Société Générale did not appear to be profiting excessively from the arrangements, (even though the price of magnesium in France in 1953 was almost double that in Canada, Norway and the United States). The Commission also expressed some misgivings about releasing SNECMA from its field-of-use restraint. On this point the Commission found that Société Générale's foundry was justified in fearing competition from a firm which, due to its ties with the state, already had certain markets reserved for it. Nonetheless, because the field-of-use restraints restricted competition in violation of Article 59 bis and did not qualify for an exemption under Article 59 ter, the Commission somewhat reluctantly removed them.

Japan

Under the FTC Guidelines, patent or know-how licensing agreements which restrict the licensee to a "specified field of technology" will not be considered to be unfair.

United States

Field-of-use restrictions have long been legal in the United States. In *General Talking Pictures v. Western Electric Co.*[92], for example, the holder of patents for electronic amplifiers created two classes of licensees distinguished by field-of-use. Fifty firms were licensed to manufacture and sell amplifiers for home use, e.g. in radios, while only two firms, both related to the patentee, were licensed to manufacture amplifiers for commercial use, here movie theatre sound systems. The case arose when one of the commercial licensees discovered a theatre employing an amplifier sold to it by a firm licensed only for the home market and sued to restrain infringement by the theatre. The Supreme Court affirmed the granting of an injunction to restrain the infringement, citing only cases holding that "patent owners may grant licences extending to all uses or limited to use in a defined field"[93]. The only limitation on this freedom is that the patentee not seek to use the licence to extend the scope of the monopoly.

A more recent decision involving field-of-use restrictions involving a product manufactured under a process patent is *United States v. Studiengesellschaft Kohle, m.b.H.*[94], where the government attacked the restrictions under Sections 1 and 2 of the Sherman Act. In that case, patents for the only economic process for making certain unpatented chemicals (aluminium trialkyls or ATAs) were held by the German firm Studiengesellshaft Kohle (SK), which originally licensed one American firm to manufacture and use ATAs in its own business and, on an exclusive basis, to sell the chemicals to others in the US. SK also licensed other firms to manufacture ATAs but restricted them to use the chemicals only in their own business; these firms had no licence to sell ATAs to others. The government attacked these field-of-use restraints as attempts to extend the process patent monopoly to the unpatented chemicals produced by it. The district court found violations of both Sections 1 and 2 as the restraints exceeded the scope of the process patent and were unlawful as both per se and unreasonable restraints of trade. The court of appeals, however, set aside both the per se and rule-of-reason determinations, finding the lower court's decision to be incorrect in distinguishing between permissible restraints on the use of a process and unpermissible restraints on the use of product produced by that process.

The court of appeals found that a per se approach drawn by such a "purely formalistic distinction" to be inappropriate under the *GTE-Sylvania* decision, which called for the use of per se prohibition only in the case of real economic effects and not because of "formalistic line drawing"[95]. Here the court of appeals found no real difference in economic effect between a restraint imposed on use of a process and a restraint imposed on the product of that process, thus a per se violation based on that distinction was incorrect. Further, the court of appeals found the restraints to be reasonable as granting additional use-restricted licences was less restrictive then the granting of just one exclusive licence. Further, the court of appeals did not find that the potential problems of field-of-use restraints to be present:

> "A number of scholars have also noted that some patent arrangements such as field-of-use restrictions have a potential for facilitating market division by giving each participant a stake in the patent in the form of an exclusive territory or by parcelling out to each competitor exclusive access to particular customers. Thus, such agreements give potential competitors incentives to remain in cartels rather than turning to another product, inventing around the patent, or challenging its validity. In this case by contrast, only Hercules (the exclusive sales licensee) enjoys any advantage from the limitation on sales, and the advantage it enjoys is far less than the advantage which a conventional exclusive licence would give it. All other competitors bound as they are by the prohibition on sales, have every incentive to compete or challenge the defendant's patent and thereby become entitled to sell ATAs."[96]

The Court found that the risk of market division was further reduced by the very strength of the patent. Market division may be a risk when there are several competing processes but it is beside the point when there is one clearly superior technology already enjoying a de facto monopoly[97].

EEC

In the EEC, field-of-use restrictions are permitted under both the patent licensing block exemption and the know-how exemption. Both exemptions find that restricting the licensee to exploitation of the technology to "one or more technical fields of application" not to be restrictive of competition within the terms of Article 85(1)[98]. The know-how exemption goes one step further and also exempts restrictions limiting the licensee to one or more product markets[99].

F.   TIE-IN SALES

Japan

In Japan, tie-in sales are the subject of case-by-case analysis under the new FTC Guidelines, and could be considered to be unfair. However, a tie-in is expressly permitted if the licensor can show that such a restriction is necessary for guaranteeing the effectiveness of the licensed technology or for maintaining the goodwill of the licensed trade mark etc. The licensor may be required to show that quality control of raw materials or components is insufficient for this purpose. In addition, in know-how licensing agreements, a tie-in sale can be permitted if the licensor can show that sucha restriction is necessary for protecting the secrecy of the licensed know-how.

Sweden

The *Sodastream*[100] case shows how the Swedish competition authorities have treated tie-ins under the Competition Act, although that case involved trade mark infringement rather than patent licensing. Sodastream sold soft-drink machines for home use which utilized refillable bottles of carbon dioxide gas. Although other firms could recharge these bottles, Sodastream required its customers to obtain refills from Sodastream and helped to finance system sales by high refill prices. NO found that Sodastream's practices were aimed at shutting out independent refillers and creating a monopoly-like position in the after-market servicing its customers. Nonetheless, NO did not find that this situation warranted intervention based on its analysis of the relevant market. NO found that the relevant market included not just home drink dispensers but soft drink sellers generally. Given keen competition in this broader market, NO saw no reason to challenge the tie-in.

United States

In the United States, the question of tie-in sales has given rise to a substantial body of case law which continues to evolve. A good starting point is the Supreme Court's 1911 decision in *Henry v. A.B. Dick Co.*[101], which upheld a patentee's right to proceed against a contributory infringer even though the patentee had tied the sale of his patented copying machines to the purchase of unpatented ink. In permitting the patentee to proceed against a

75

competing ink seller, the Court rejected the argument that the tie was being used to extend the patentee's monopoly power to an unpatented article. Instead, the Court viewed the tie-in as simply a different way for the patentee to collect the profits to which it was entitled in any event and noted that the patentee was selling its machines at or below cost.

Judicial tolerance of tie-ins did not last long; *A.B. Dick* was overruled five years later in *Motion Picture Patents Co. v. Universal Film Manufacturing Co.*[102]. That case involved an infringement action by the holder of patents on a certain movie projector design against the producer, distributor and exhibitor of certain movies. The patented projectors, evidently the only workable projectors at the time, were sold subject to a requirement that they be used only to show unpatented film supplied by the patentee, thus the claim of infringement against film coming from third parties. Here, however, the Court upheld lower court decisions dismissing the infringement action due to the tie-in. Overruling *A.B. Dick*, the Court held that the restriction was invalid because patentee was seeking to extend his patent monopoly in projectors to the markets for film production and use. The fact that the projectors were provided at cost was seen not as a benefit as in *A.B. Dick* but as proof of the very evil complained of, the taking of profits on the unpatented supplies.

While *Motion Picture Patents* thus represents a sharp swing away from the decision in *A. B. Dick*, it can perhaps be explained by the intervening passage of the Clayton Act, Section 3 of which prohibited tie-in sales which may substantially restrain trade. Although *Motion Picture Patents* was not a Clayton Act case, the Court did cite the Act and was influenced by that expression of congressional intent[103].

A number of infringement cases reaching the Supreme Court in the decades following *Motion Picture Patents* were decided in a similar and summary fashion if the patentee was engaged in any kind of tying, even for what seems now to be clearly metering purposes. In *Morton Salt Co. v. G.S. Suppiger Co.*[104], for example, Suppiger tried to enjoin the infringement of its patent on salt tablet dispensing machines used in canning by Morton, which leased similar unpatented machines. The Supreme Court held that Suppiger could not obtain an injunction because of its "unclean hands" in tying the purchase of salt tablets to the machine leases. The equitable clean hands doctrine was applied because the Court found that the tie-in suppressed competition in the salt tablet market, but without discussing in any fashion the nature of that market or how competition would be reduced.

The Court reached a similar result in *B.B. Chemical Co. v. Ellis*[105], decided the same day as *Morton Salt*. In *B.B. Chemical*, the owner of a patented process for reinforcing shoe insoles supplied shoe manufacturers with the unpatented materials needed to utilise the process (fabric and glue) and sought to enjoin the infringement of another firm which supplied similar materials. The patentee made no charge to its licensees for use of the process and likewise supplied free of charge certain machinery and glue, charging only for fabric. While the Court recognised the convenience of the arrangement, it held that the firm had restrained competition by creating a "limited monopoly" in its unpatented materials and thus could not restrain the infringement.

Two years later, the Supreme Court again struck down a patent licensing arrangement which involved a tie-in on an unpatented product. That case involved two companion decisions, *Mercoid Corp. v. Mid-Continent Investment Co. (Mercoid I)*[106] and *Mercoid Corp. v. Minneapolis-Honeywell Regulation Co. (Mercoid II)*[107], arising out of a patent for a forced-air heating system. Mid-Continent held the patent on the system design and Honeywell was its exclusive licensee. Honeywell did not manufacture the heating system itself, however; it made only the unpatented controls necessary for the system to function. It sub-licensed five firms to make and sell the system on condition that they buy their controls from Honeywell. All royalty payments between the sub-licensees and Honeywell and between Honeywell and the licensor were based on sales of the controls. Mercoid was sued for contributory infringement, as it made and sold switches which would permit other firms to infringe the patented heating system. Mercoid defended based on misuse of the patent by seeking to extend it to the non-patented switches and counterclaimed for treble damages. In the companion case, Mercoid sued Honeywell to have another heating system patent declared invalid because of misuse and again for treble damages for antitrust violations.

The Supreme Court found misuse in both cases based on the asserted efforts by Mid-Continent and Honeywell to extend their patent monopolies to the unpatented controls, brushing aside Honeywell's claim that it was merely charging according to the number of heating systems sold by its sub-licensees. The opinions do not make at all clear how competition was harmed by the practice. Indeed, the exact relationship between Honeywell and its sub-licensees is murky in the opinions, as the Court states that Honeywell did not manufacture or sell heating systems but also refers to the five firms as Honeywell's "manufacturing competitors"[108]. Rather than analyse these relationships and determine how competition might be harmed, the opinions engage in rhetoric about the dangers of such tie-ins, calling the case "a graphic illustration of the evils of an expansion of the patent monopoly by private engagements" and expressing fears that "such a vast power to multiply monopolies ... at the will of the patentee would carve out exceptions to the antitrust laws which Congress has not sanctioned"[109].

An example of public enforcement in a tying case is *International Salt Co. v. United States*[110], decided four years after the *Mercoid* decisions. In *International Salt*, the government sought an injunction against alleged violation of Section 1 of the Sherman Act and Section 3 of the Clayton Act for International Salt's use of tying contracts in its leasing of patented salt-dispensing machines. These contracts required the lessees to purchase all salt used in the machines from International Salt.

The case gives another example of how abbreviated the Court's analysis became when a tie-in was used in connection with a patented product. Here the Court found the tie-in to be a per se violation because it foreclosed competitors from a "substantial market", here $500 000 in annual sales of salt. According to the Court, "The volume of business affected by these contracts cannot be said to be insignificant or insubstantial and the tendencies of the arrangements to accomplishment of monopoly seems obvious"[111]. The Court was unmoved by defence claims that the tie-in assured salt of high purity, important given defendant's machine maintenance obligations (a specification system was suggested instead) and that the defendant's contract terms obliged it to meet any rival offers (the tie-in still stifled competition)[112].

More recent decisions by the Supreme Court showing an increasing sensitivity to some of the economic bases for tying contracts. In 1980, the Court decided *Dawson Chemical Co. v. Rohm and Haas Co.*[113], in which it interpreted amendments to the Patent Act seeking to give patentees some measure of control over non-staple non-patented goods used with the patented invention. The question specifically was whether a tying contract involving the non-staple fell within the statute, thereby preserving the patentee's right to sue for contributory infringement without being charged with "misuse" for the tie-in. (In that case, Rohm and Haas had developed a patented process for spraying the chemical propanil on rice crops. Propanil was unpatented and had no other uses at the time. Dawson sold propanil as well, along with instructions to farmers on how to employ Rohm and Haas' patented technique.) The Supreme Court in a 5-4 decision read the statute in a way which effectively permits tie-ins in such situations. In reaching that result, the majority noted that denying Rohm and Haas the ability to act against contributory infringers because of the misuse of a tie-in would substantially reduce the incentive for firms to invest in research. Here costly research was necessary for the discovery of new uses for the myriad chemical compounds already in existence[114].

The Supreme Court's most recent treatment of tie-ins occurred not in the context of patent licensing but in the sale of hospital services. The case nonetheless indicates current thinking on the Court which is directly applicable to know-how licensing and gives some indication of how patent licensing tie-ins would be treated. In that case, *Jefferson Parish Hospital Dist. No. 2 v. Hyde*[115], the Court considered a private antitrust action brought by Dr. Hyde, an anaethesiologist, alleging a violation of Section 1 of the Sherman Act by the hospital and others. The alleged violation arose out of the hospital's contracting with another firm to provide anaesthesiology services to the hospital. This exclusive contract, according to Hyde, was a tie-in by the hospital (surgery being provided only in conjunction with the services of the hospital's own anaesthesiologist) and, because the hospital had power in the local market, it was a per se violation of Section 1. The district court denied relief to Dr. Hyde but the court of appeals reversed, find a per se violation based on the tie-in. The Supreme Court reversed again, finding the tie-in reasonable. Although all nine justices agreed with that result, they split five-four on how to analyse tie-ins. The majority continued to apply existing case law, that a tie-in by a firm with market power was per se unlawful, but found that there was no market power in the present case and that the tie-in was reasonable under the facts. In reaching that decision the majority reiterated that tie-ins by firms with market power were per se unlawful because they permit anticompetitive "forcing" of the tied product on the purchaser. The majority thus distinguished between merely raising the price of the tying product and what it saw as the suppression of competition in the market for the tied product. The danger, according to the majority, was in the potential harm to existing competitors and raising of barriers to entry to new competitors. The metering aspect of tie-ins was seen not as a benefit but as increasing the social costs of market power by increasing monopoly profits[116].

The majority then turned to the question of market power. Although the majority ultimately found that market power was lacking here and per se illegality thus inappropriate, it listed three circumstances in which it would continue to apply per se treatment: when the product was unique, commanded a high market share or was patented[117]. Concerning patents, the majority said it was "fair to presume" market power based on the patent and that "any effort to enhance the scope of the patent monopoly" through a tie-in would undermine "competition on the merits" in the market for the tied good[118].

The four justices who concurred in the result took exception both to continued per se treatment of any tie-ins and to the presumption of market power for patented goods.

The minority opinion argued that per se treatment is inappropriate because a tie-in does not generally increase the profits which a seller with market power can obtain by selling the tying product; the creation of additional market power in the tied good (an "extension of market power") was seen as unlikely unless three conditions are found: (1) power in the tying product market; (2) an ability to gain power in the tied-product market (depending on market structure and entry conditions); and (3) a "coherent economic basis" for treating the two products as distinct[119]. These three criteria would only be threshhold requirements under the minority's view. The rule of reason analysis would then have to consider the possible economic benefits of tie-ins, including facilitating new entry, permitting clandestine price-cutting, protecting goodwill and reducing costs through "economies of joint production and distribution"[120]. Notably, the minority disputed the majority's view of the metering function of tie-ins. The minority, citing Bork, argued that price discrimination through a metering tie-in reduces rather than increases the economic costs of market power[121]. Further, and of particular interest here, the minority disputed the majority's statement that a presumption of market power is merited when a product is patented, stating that "a patent holder has no market power in any relevant sense if there are close substitutes for the patented product"[122].

This decision in Jefferson Parish, while not dealing with patented goods and not, as yet, changing the law applicable to tie-ins, does show that there is considerable ferment within the Court on the issue.

Further, given the Court's increasing appreciation of the pro-competitive effects of many vertical restraints and corresponding reluctance to continue unjustified per se prohibitions (e.g., the very recent *Sharp Electronics* opinion, written by a justice new to the Court since *Jefferson Parish*), it seems likely that a tie-in rule similar to the one argued for by the minority may become the law in the near future.

EEC

The position taken by the Commission against tie-in clauses in cases reviewing licensing contracts has continued consistently in its licensing regulations. In its decision in *Vaessen/Morris*[123], for example, the Commission came down against licensing contracts which tied the use of a patented sausage-stuffing machine to the purchase of unpatented sausage casings from the licensor.

In that case, Morris held Belgian patents for a process and machine to manufacture "saucisson de Boulogne", a local speciality. These inventions permitted the use of thinner casings and saved 75 per cent of the labour previously required to make this sausage. Morris licensed local sausage manufacturers and supplied them with his machine free of charge provided that they purchased their casings from him. Vaessen was a competing casing manufacturer which complained of its inability to sell like-quality casings in this market.

In finding a restriction on trade within the meaning of Article 85(1), the Commission relied upon the inability of sausage makers to choose their suppliers and the inability of Vaessen to penetrate this particular market. The market, moreover, was narrowly defined as the market for "saucisson de Boulogne" casings rather than sausage casings generally. (While Morris held a two-thirds share of the casing market in this speciality, it held only five per cent of the overall casing market.) The opinion does not discuss entry conditions in the market for this special casing but Vaessen did produce it and presumably other manufacturers could do so as well.

The Commission found the tie-in not to be a "requirement imposed by the industrial property right" because it believed that Morris could exploit his patent without tying casing sales. The Commission thus found the tie-in to be "an unlawful extension by contractual means of the monopoly given by the patent"[124].

The Commission further found the agreement not to qualify for an exemption under Article 85(3) for two reasons. First, the tie-in was not seen as improving production or promoting technical progress but as impeding progress, impeded because the sausage makers' freedom of action was limited and because they could not buy less expensive casings. Further, the use of Morris' casings was not necessary to the proper exploitation of the patent, as Vaessen's casings worked well in Morris' machines[125].

Tie-ins receive similarly negative treatment under both the patent licensing block exemption and under the know-how exemption. Under Article 2(1)(1) of the patent regulation, tie-ins are exempt only if "necessary for a technically satisfactory exploitation of the licensed invention". Further, Article 3(9) removes from the block exemption entirely any agreement where the licensee is "induced" to accept goods or services "he does not want" unless again "necessary for a technically satisfactory exploitation of the licensed invention". The know-how regulation follows the same pattern in its Articles 2(1)(5) and 3(3), but it also permits tie-ins necessary for insuring that the licensee's production conforms to quality standards followed by the licensor and other licensees.

G. PACKAGE LICENSING

Cases dealing with package licensing are closely related conceptually to the cases on tie-ins presented above. They are also related to some of the cases dealing with royalty terms set forth in the Part H below, in particular to cases involving the licensing of multiple patents which expire at different points during the licensing contract. Despite these overlaps and similarities, we try to single out in this part cases dealing specifically with the licensing of several patents as a package.

Japan

In Japan, package licensing is the subject of case-by-case analysis, and can be found to be unfair under the new FTC Guidelines. However, it is expressly permitted when package licensing is necessary for guaranteeing the effectiveness of the licensed technology.

United States

In the United States, package licensing of patents does not offend the antitrust laws or give rise to patent misuse if the licensor has not "forced" the package upon the licensee. The Supreme Court has recognised that where numerous patents are involved, the parties may wish to treat them as a block and establish a simplified royalty system for their mutual convenience, as in the *Automatic Radio*[126] case discussed in the next part.

An application of this concept can be seen in *American Securit Co. v. Shatterproof Glass Corp.*[127], which involved a group of patents for the production of tempered flat glass. Securit had offered Shatterproof a package of licences at a royalty rate fixed on the quantity of glass produced and without regard to the number of patents actually used. When Shatterproof complained about the package arrangement, it was offered individual patents but at the same royalty rate. Shatterproof rejected this offer and began producing without any licence. In Securit's subsequent suit for infringement, the court considered whether Shatterproof's offers, characterised by the court as mandatory package licensing, amounted to per se patent misuse which would block the action for infringement. The court of appeals found that it did because Securit had sought to use one patent as a "lever" to force Shatterproof to accept other licences[128].

A contrasting result can be seen in *Western Electric. Co. v. Stewart-Warner Corp.*[129] showing how a licensor can avoid a charge of patent misuse by offering a part of the package at a different price, even if the terms offered prove unacceptable to the would-be licensee. In that case, Stewart-Warner sought a licence under a certain patent for use in semiconductor manufacturing. Western Electric's initial offer was to license any or all of its semiconductor patents. Later, it offered a deal for all of its patents at a reduced royalty rate provided that Stewart-Warner grant back royalty-free a licence under its own patents. Stewart-Warner's counter offer was to license only the one Western Electric patent which it wanted. In payment, it offered royalties plus the royalty-free grantback of its own patents. Western Electric refused this, saying that it would take the grantback as part payment only if Stewart-Warner took the complete package of patents. Instead, it offered the single patent at a certain royalty rate with no grantback.

In the subsequent action for patent infringement, Stewart-Warner alleged patent misuse as a defence, claiming that Western Electric tried to coerce a package licence by refusing to take the grantback as part payment in the proposed single patent licence. The court of appeals disagreed and distinguished the *American Securit* decision. Here, Western Electric did offer the single patent and at a different royalty rate than for the package. Because it had offered Stewart-Warner a choice on reasonable terms, albeit not the terms Stewart-Warner wanted, it had not engaged in patent misuse.

EEC

In the EC, the question of package licences is treated under Article 3(9) of patent licensing block exemption and Article 3(3) of the know-how exemption. "Inducing" a licensee to accept an additional licence which he "does not want" and which is not "necessary for a technically satisfactory exploitation of the licensed invention" removes the entire agreement from the protection of the block exemption. Package licensing can also be imposed under the know-how regulation if necessary to ensure quality standards followed by the licensor or other licensees.

H.   ROYALTY TERMS

Two main issues are found in connection with the royalty terms of licensing agreement. The first relates to setting royalties according to output or total sales, which may include products not using the licensed technology or products using a changing mix of licensed technology as patents expire during the course of the agreement (issues closely related to the question of package licensing above). The second major type of issue, and overlapping with the first, relates to the charging of royalties on unpatented products, unpatented either because the patent has expired or because it was never issued. Given the similarity of the issues, cases dealing with both issues are presented here.

Germany

In a case decided in 1962 "*Puder*" the Federal Court held that any contractual agreement to pay royalties after the expiry of the protected right (in the case of a trade secret after the secret has become public knowledge) would extend the scope of that right and therefore be invalid under Section 20 of the ARC[130]. This would not apply in cases involving payment methods for royalties accruing after the protected period.

In its decision of 30th September 1981 *"Windsurfing"* the Federal Cartel Office prohibited the extension of various clauses of a licensing agreement including the royalty terms to unprotected parts of a composite product[131].

Windsurfing International, a company established under Californian law is the holder of a German patent for rigs on windsurfing boards. It concluded licensing agreements for the production and sale of windsurf boards on the German market providing, inter alia, that the patented rigs could only be used for standard boards approved by the licensor, that rigs and boards could only be sold as a unit and that the royalty would be assessed on the net sales price of the windsurfer consisting of the patented rig and the unpatented board.

The decision of the FCO first discussed the scope of the protected right holding that a functional link between the rig and the board was not sufficient to extend the protection of the patent to the unpatented part. The clause requiring licensor approval for the use of the board was held to exceed the scope of the protected right, which was limited to the rig. Finally, the assessment of the royalty on the basis of the net sales price of the total product (composed of patented and unpatented parts) was considered a restriction exceeding the scope of the protected right. The FCO rejected the licensor arguments that this was a method of payment designed to provide an easy and efficient way to meter the royalties to be paid under the contract. In its view, the value relationship between rig and board fluctuated according to factors independent from the value of the protected component, which therefore should be the only appropriate measure for metering payments.

Japan

Under the FTC's Guidelines, basing royalty payments on the price of the final product will not be considered to be unfair in either patent or know-how licensing contracts if certain conditions are met. In particular, the final product must require the use of the licensed technology, whether in a production process of or for a component of the finished product. Where royalties are charged on products or services other than the licensed goods, the agreement may be found to be unfair. The Guidelines apply the above distinctions to both patent and know-how licensing agreements, but distinguish between patents and know-how for other royalty-related terms. In particular, patent licensing agreements which charge royalties after the expiration of the patent rights are considered to be unfair, but know-how licensors will have somewhat more flexibility. Know-how licensing agreements will not be considered to be unfair if they provide for royalties to continue for "a short period" during the term of the agreement but after the know-how has become publicly known. If the licensee is the source of the disclosure, however, royalty payments apparently may be required for the life of the agreement.

United States

A good starting point in the United States is *Automatic Radio Mfg. co. v. Hazeltine Research Inc.*[132], which involved a package licensing agreement covering hundreds of radio patents. The agreement established a minimum annual royalty and additional payments based on the number of radios manufactured, whether or not they employed any of the licensed technology. When Hazeltine sued for royalties, patent misuse was raised as a defence. The Court did not, however, apply a per se rule as it found that such an agreement would not necessarily extend the patent monopoly. Further, it found that setting royalties according to a licensee's total sales to be reasonable since "sound business judgment could indicate that such payment represents the most convenient method" of fixing the value of the agreement[133].

Automatic Radio was narrowed, however, in Zenith Radio Corp. v. Hazeltine Research, Inc.[134]. In Zenith, Hazeltine had again offered a package licence with royalties to be fixed on total sales. Here, however, the Supreme Court found misuse because it found that the clause was not for the convenience of the parties but was due instead to Hazeltine alone. Applying notions of patent extension and leverage, the Court held that it was misuse for the patentee to insist upon a percentage-of-sales royalty, regardless of the actual use of the licensed patents. The Court held that the licensee could "insist upon paying only for use, and not upon the basis of total sales"[135].

The Supreme Court's position on post-expiration royalties was set out in Brulotte v. Thys Co.[136], which involved an action for non-payment of royalties on certain harvesting machines. The machines incorporated seven patents, all of which had expired. The issue before the Court was whether royalties could be collected after the expiration of all seven patents. The Court found seeking royalties beyond the expiration of all patents to be misuse per se, preventing the collection of royalties for that period, because the patentee was seeking "to project its monopoly beyond the patent period"[137].

Notably, the Court asserted, without explanation, that this practice was "wholly different" from the use of long-term payments to finance the sale of an unpatented machine. A dissenting opinion questioned this, arguing that the transaction involved both the licence of a patented idea and the lease of a machine. While use of the idea could not be controlled after the expiration of the patent, others could then imitate it. Machinery, however, was different; the dissent saw no reason why the machinery could not continue to be subject to restrictions in the same way that unpatented machinery could be restricted. Because a long term payment contract would be permitted on an unpatented machine, the dissent believed that post-expiration royalties on Thys' machine should similarly be permitted[138].

A variation on the facts of Brulotte v. Thys can be seen in Rockform Corp. v. Acitelli-Standard Concrete Wall Inc.[139], which involved the licensing of a package of patents related to a form for pouring concrete basement walls. The licensor licensed numerous construction firms to use this system, supplying materials and charging a fee for each basement built using the system. In its suit for infringement, Rockform was charged with patent misuse by Actelli for creating a package of licences, only one of which was important, and not providing for a reduction in royalties following the expiration of the important patent. The court of appeals agreed, finding that such a grouping of patents without a clause allowing the licensee to terminate amounted to an unlawful effort to extend the about-to-expire patent[140].

Similar facts produced a more nuanced opinion in Beckman Instruments Inc. v. Technical Development Corp.[141], which involved a package of sub-licences with royalties paid on gross sales of various categories of products. The agreement was to continue until the expiration of the last patent sub-licensed, unless the sub-licensee terminated the agreement for non-use of any patent and quit the field of use. The court of appeals held that an arrangement continuing until the last patent expired could be valid, provided that the agreement was not coerced. Improper "conditioning" under Zenith, however, would mark the agreement as an unjustified extension of the patent monopoly[142].

A final example of the treatment of royalty terms in the US is Miller Insituform v. Insituform of North America[143], which concerned a sub-licence for the use of a process to renovate sewer pipes. A suit by a terminated sub-licensee alleged, inter alia, that the royalty formula, a percentage of the sub-licensee's total sales, amounted to patent misuse because the percentage applied to unpatented work as well as to work under the process patent. The trial court disagreed and distinguished the decisions in *Automatic Radio* and *Zenith* as involving situations where some products were not covered by patents. Here, every job which the licensee undertook included at one stage the use of the patented process. Having thus distinguished *Zenith* and *Automatic Radio*, the court saw no need to determine whether "conditioning" had occurred and, because the bargaining had been at arm's length, the court would not second guess the formula which had been created[144].

The DOJ Guidelines take a completly different approach to royalty terms in licensing agreements. According to the Guidelines:

"The Department generally is not concerned with the amount of licence royalties or the basis upon which licence royalties are measured. As a general matter, licensees will pay for the licensed technology no more than what they think the technology is worth. Moreover, various types of royalty payment provisions (for example, package licensing and royalties paid on sales of products made from a patented process) can encourage licensees to develop and promote the licensed technology efficiently by enabling the licensee to use the technology in combination with other inputs in order to produce the final product at the lowest possible cost. In particular, a royalty provision based on total unit sales of a product regardless of whether it is made using the licensed technology may save licensors the costs of determining how much its licensees' production utilizes the licensed technology. Finally, calculating a royalty on the basis of a licensee's use of some complementary input or inputs on the basis of the sales of some downstream products can be used to meter differences in demand for the technology among different licensees. In this way, the licensor may be able to disseminate its technology more widely than if it had to charge a fixed royalty rate."[145]

EEC

One Commission decision touching on the imposition of royalties on unpatented products is *AOIP/Beyrard*[146], in which the French inventor Beyrard licensed AOIP to manufacture a number of patented electrical devices. One clause of the agreement permitted Beyrard to extend its term by the inclusion of subsequently obtained patents or improvements patents. AOIP was obligated to continue paying royalties even if all of the original patents had expired and no use was being made of new patents later obtained by Beyrard.

The Commission found this clause to fall within Article 85(1) as it burdened the manufacturer with additional costs with no economic justification. The Commission took particular exception to the fact that Beyrard could extend the agreement unilaterally while AOIP could not for its part terminate it.

The Commission found a further violation of Article 85(1) in the fact that AOIP was, during the original term of the agreement, obligated to pay royalties on the types of products covered by the agreement even if none of Beyrard's patents was actually used. This restricted competition in the same fashion as the unilateral extension clause, in that payments would be required with no economic basis. Further, competition in research and development was restricted in that AOIP, bound to pay royalties in any event, had a reduced incentive in performing its own research or in using the inventions of third parties[147].

The Commission's approach in *AOIP/Beyrard* is carried over into the patent-licensing block exemption. Article 3(2) denies the benefits of the exemption to any agreement containing an automatic extension clause for subsequent patents unless each party has the right to terminate once the originally-licensed patents have expired. That article permits, however, the licensor to continue collecting royalties on still non-public know-how utilized by the licensee following the expiration of the original patents.

Article 3(4) of that exemption gives similar treatment to agreements charging royalties on unpatented products, products not produced by a patented process or products produced by using no longer secret know-how (and not made public by the licensee). An exception, however, is provided to permit payment terms extended beyond the life of the patent or secret know-how.

Parallel treatment is given in the know-how exemption. Article 3(5) excludes agreements which charge royalties on goods not produced using the licensed technology or using it after it has been made public by the licensor in violation of the agreement. Article 2(1)(7), however, places the risks of other disclosure of the know-how on the licensee. That provision exempts obligations to continue paying royalties to the end of the agreement in the event that the know-how becomes publicly known and further permits damages if the disclosure is the fault of the licensee. Article 3(10) excludes from the block exemption agreements which can be unilaterally extended beyond that period through the transmission of additional know-how, unless the licensee can refuse the improvements or terminate at the expiry of the initial term of the agreement and at least every three years thereafter. Under Article 7(7), the benefits of the block exemption can be withdrawn where an obligation to continue paying royalties following disclosure, otherwise permitted under Article 2(1)(7), "substantially exceeds" the lead time gained by the licensee and the obligation to pay "is detrimental to competition in the market".

I.   GRANTBACKS

Japan

The FTC's Guidelines give identical treatment to patent and know-how grantback terms. If the licensing agreement requires an assignment or exclusive grantback of the new technology to the licensor, the FTC will consider that requirement highly likely to be unfair, given the possible "undue enhancement or maintenance of a dominant position" and the negative effects on licensee incentives to engage in R & D. Agreements which require non-exclusive grantbacks to the licensor of improvements or informing the licensor of knowledge or experience gained with the licensed technology may be considered to be unfair if "unduly disadvantageous" to the licensee. Balanced grantback agreements, however, will not be considered to be unfair, that is, agreements which provide mutual obligations on the licensor and licensee to inform the other of new knowledge or experience and to grant non-exclusive licences in improvements and which are "roughly balanced in substance".

United States

In the United States, the decision in *Transparent-Wrap Machine Corp. v. Stokes and Smith Co.*[148] established that grantback clauses in patent licensing contracts will be reviewed under the rule of reason rather than held to a standard of per se illegality. In that case,

Transparent-Wrap sold to Stokes an exclusive licence to manufacture and sell patented packaging machines on the condition, inter alia, that the licensee assign all improvements patents to the licensor. When Stokes failed to later assign certain patents, Transparent-Wrap attempted to terminate the licence.

In considering whether Transparent-Wrap should be enjoined from enforcing that clause, the Supreme Court noted the potential for grantback clauses to cause anticompetitive effects:

"We are quite aware of the possibilities of abuse in the practice of licensing a patent on condition that the licensee assign all improvement patents to the licensor. Conceivably the device could be employed with the purpose or effect of violating the antitrust laws. He who acquires two patents acquires a double monopoly. As patents are added to patents a whole industry may be regimented. The owner of a basic patent might thus perpetuate his control over an industry long after the basic patent expired. Competitors might be eliminated and an industrial monopoly perfected and maintained. Through the use of patent pools or multiple licensing agreements the fruits of invention of an entire industry might be systematically funnelled into the hands of the original patentee."[149]

Despite this potential for harm, the Court held that per se illegality was inappropriate given that the Patent Act specifically makes all patents assignable[150].

The recent Justice Department Guidelines take a considerably more positive view of grantback clauses:

"A grantback feature in a patent licence also is often procompetitive, especially if it is non-exclusive. Where practising a patent is likely to lead to further innovations in the patented technology (whether or not such innovations are patentable), a grantback may enable a patentee to avoid the possibility that such innovation by the licensee will either make obsolete the patentee's own technology or effectively prevent the patentee from itself developing further improvements in its technology. A grantback also may serve to compensate the patentee for improvements developed by the licensee that the licensee could not have developed without access to the patentee's technology. ... [A] grantback could also increase the efficiency of bargaining for a licence. The grantback might function as consideration to the patentee in a contract to exploit the licensed technology. In that case, the price would be determined ex ante (in the form of a grantback), rather than ex post (after the improvements exist), when bargaining would be complicated by the parties' bilateral monopolies. Using a grantback to facilitate bargaining would directly benefit the parties and ultimately would also benefit consumers."[151]

EEC

The Commission's enforcement policy with respect to grantback clauses has been relatively consistent over the years, including both cases and the two block exemptions. For example, in 1972, in the *Raymond/Nagoya* decision[152] the Commission approved a patent licensing agreement which required Nagoya to grantback to Raymond non-exclusive licences for patented improvements in Raymond's processes as well as non-exclusive licences for new patents in this field but unrelated to Raymond's technology. Further, each party was obligated to inform each other of improvements in using the process during the life of the agreement. The Commission decision noted that the grantback provisions, being non-exclusive, did not prevent Nagoya from granting other licences in the EEC and thus did not restrict competition within Article 85(1). (The parties had dropped an earlier exclusive grantback provision at the Commission's suggestion.) Further, the continuing exchange of information concerning improvements and other know-how was considered to be "part and parcel of the contractual utilisation property rights and know-how" created by the agreement and thus was not a restriction of competition with Article 85(1).

In *Kabelmetal/Luchaire*[153], slightly different facts were presented concerning a grantback clause. There, the licensee was obligated to grantback improvements on a non-exclusive basis to Kabelmetal, just as in *Raymond/Nagoya*, but Kabelmetal reserved the right to sublicense these improvements to others. The Commission was concerned that this right to sublicense would limit Luchaire's incentive to innovate, as it would effectively lose control over its innovation. Nonetheless, the Commission decided that the arrangement did not substantially restrict competition under the terms of Article 85(1) given the hypothetical nature of the problem. (Kabelmetal at the time had no other licensees.)[154]

The patent licensing block exemption treats grantback clauses in a similar fashion as found in the cases summarized above. Under Article 2(1)(10), mutual obligation to communicate improvements and to grantback non-exclusive licences are not restrictive of competition under Article 85(1). Article 3(8), however, removes from the block exemption any agreement which obliges a licensee to "assign wholly or in part" improvements or new applications patents to the licensor.

The know-how exemption contains similar but more elaborate grantback provisions than the patent regulation. Article 2(1)(4) finds that mutual obligations to communicate experience and exchange licences for improvements or new applications are not restrictive of competition but only if certain conditions are met. First, the licensee must be free to license its improvements to others, provided that it does not divulge still secret licensor know-how. Second, the grantback licence to the licensor must not run past the period of the original licence. According to Article 3(2)(a), an obligation on the licensee to "assign" its improvements or new applications removes the agreement from the block exemption. Article 3(2) goes further, however, (and thus helps to explain the patent exemption) by also prohibiting exclusive grantbacks to the licensor which would prevent the licensee from using its improvement or licensing it to a third party. Further, under Article 3(2)(c) grantback agreements are prohibited which, even if non-exclusive and reciprocal, give the licensor use of the improvement beyond the period in which the licensee may use the original know-how.

J. NO CHALLENGES

Canada

In the unreported decision in *R. v. Union Carbide Ltd. et al.* discussed in Part E above, one of the clauses objected to as a patent abuse in violation of Section 29 required licensees not to challenge the validity of patents on plastic film-treating machinery even after the expiration of the licensing agreements. In the negotiated settlement, Carbide agreed to drop, inter alia, the no-challenge provision from its licences.

Japan

The FTC's Guidelines provide that it is not unfair for a licensor to provide for termination of the licensing agreement in the event of a licensee challenge, but that it may be unfair for the licensor to prohibit challenges outright in the licensing agreement.

United States

In the *United States*, the ability of a licensee to challenge a patent was clearly established in *Lear v. Adkins*[155], which held that a licensee was not estopped by virtue of its licence to bring a challenge. In making that determination, the Supreme Court found that the patentee's equities did not weigh very heavily against the public interest in "full and free competition in the use of ideas which are in reality part of the public domain"[156]. The Court noted that licensees typically were the only parties with enough economic incentive to bring a challenge and if they could be prevented from doing so, the costs associated with unjustified patent grants would continue[157].

EEC

The Commission has consistently found no-challenge clauses to be restrictive of competition within Article 85(1) beginning with decisions in the early 1970s and continuing through the current block exemptions. In the *Vaessen/Morris* sausage casing decision, for example, the Commission found that the no-challenge clause restrained competition by preventing the licensee from acting to remove "an obstacle to his freedom of action"[158]. The Commission was unsympathetic to the dilemma thus created for the patentee, that information he provides to his licensee might be used against him, given the public interest in the revocation of wrongly issued patents[159]. On the other hand, the Commission did not require the elimination of a no-challenge clause in *Raymond/Nagoya*[160] given that the restriction on Nagoya was seen to restrain trade only in Nagoya's Asian markets and not in the EEC. The Commission does not discuss why its interest in seeking invalid patents overturned is not compelling when the licensee is outside the EEC, but this anomaly is perhaps explained by the fact that *Raymond/Nagoya* was decided before *Vaessen/Morris*.

No contest clauses receive similar treatment under both block exemptions. Under Article 3(1) of the patent exemption, a no-challenge clause removes a licensing agreement from the block exemption. Article 3(1) permits, however, a licensor to terminate the licence in the event of a challenge. Article 2(1)(8) further protects the licensee's ability to challenge by permitting the imposition of obligations on the licensee to act against infringers only if the licensee's right to challenge is preserved. Articles 3(4) and 2(1)(7) of the know-how exemption is similar with respect to preserving the licensee's right to challenge the secrecy of the know-how.

In its recent decision *Bayer/Süllhöfer*[161], the Court of Justice took up the question of no contest clauses for the first time. In that case Bayer and Süllhöfer possessed conflicting patents and registered designs for processes and machinery used in the production of polyurethane foam panels. This conflict led to litigation in which Bayer challenged Süllhöfer's utility model and patent application as well as Süllhöfer's infringement claim. That litigation was settled by a non-exclusive cross-licensing agreement. While Süllhöfer licensed to Bayer royalty-free, it agreed to pay Bayer substantial royalties for the licence it received. Bayer, for its part, agreed not to challenge the Süllhöfer patent.

A subsequent disagreement led Süllhöfer to challenge the agreement in the German courts. After the Dusseldorf Court of Appeals (*Oberlandesgericht*) found the no contest clause invalid under Article 85(1) of the Rome Treaty, the question of validity under Article 85(1) was submitted to the Court of Justice by the German Federal Court.

The Court's opinion found that no challenge clauses could, as a result of legal or market conditions, restrict competition in violation of Article 85(1). In reaching this conclusion the Court eliminated two broad categories of agreements as possible violations. In the first are agreements containing no contest clauses but which do not involve the payment of royalties. The other category involves agreements which include the payment of substantial royalties but which involve an outmoded technology. The Court went on to find that the remaining category, involving current technology and substantial royalties, could restrain trade but that the national court would still be required to go on to decide whether the agreement involved a significant lessening of competition, based on an examination of the market position of the parties.

In reaching its decision the Court focused exclusively on the degree of restriction imposed on the licensee, disregarding the fact that an invalid patent, even if licensed free of charge to one firm, can still restrain competition vis-à-vis third parties. It rejected a different formulation proposed by the Commission. Under that formulation, no contest clauses would have been viewed as possibly restrictive of competition but acceptable as compatible with Article 85(1) if part of the settlement of good faith litigation relating to the challenged right and the settlement did not include other restrictive agreements.

K.   POOLING AND CROSS-LICENSING

The pooling or cross-licensing of patents can be used by the grantors or licensors to obtain many of the anticompetitive objectives touched upon in earlier parts of this chapter, e.g., a pool could be used in an effort to fix prices, limit output or assign territories or fields of use. Thus there is a natural overlap with the cases already discussed. Pools, however, merit separate treatment as they pose increased risk of collusion among competitors, while the previous parts dealt primarily with issues of vertical restraints.

United States

In the United States two Supreme Court decisions, neither of them recent, give good examples of the major issues in the analysis of patent pools under US law. The first decision is *Standard Oil Co. v. United States*[162], which involved a government challenge under Sections 1 and 2 of the Sherman Act to a patent pool created during the 1920s related to processes for refining gasoline. Four companies had developed competing, patented processes for gaining additional "cracked" gasoline during refining and were engaged in litigation over claims of infringement. This litigation was settled by the creation of a patent pool which permitted each firm to use the patents in question. Moreover, each firm could sublicense the pooled patents as well as license its own, with royalties to be shared among the pool members. Forty-six firms had been licensed by the four members of the pool.

The Supreme Court reversed a decision that the pool violated the Sherman Act. While recognising the potential of a pool to dominate an industry and to fix prices by fixing royalty rates, the Court held that "cross-licensing and division of royalties violates the act only when used to effect a monopoly, or to fix prices or to impose otherwise an unreasonable restraint upon interstate commerce"[163]. Here, there was no showing of restraint of trade. The pool and its licensees accounted for only 55 per cent of cracked gasoline capacity, given a proliferation of other processes. Further, at the time cracked gasoline itself accounted for only 26 per cent of all gasoline production. Thus, no monopoly or restraint of trade was shown by the pool.

The Court was also sensitive to the fact that infringement claims led to the pool's creation in the first place:

"Where there are legitimately conflicting claims or threatened interferences, a settlement by agreement, rather than litigation, is not precluded by the Act. An interchange of patent rights and a division of royalties according to the value attributed by the parties to their respective patent claims are frequently necessary if technical advancement is not to be blocked by threatened litigation. If the available advantages are open on reasonable terms to all manufacturers desiring to participate, such interchange may promote rather than restrain competition."[164]

A contrasting example can be seen in *Hartford-Empire Co. v. United States*[165], which involved a patent pool utilized to cartelize the glass container industry. In that case, patents for the "gob" process of making glassware were largely in the hands of one firm, Hartford-Empire, but additional and possibly infringing gob-related patents were held by competing manufacturers. Litigation over the claimed infringements was settled by licensing agreements. The firms did not stop there, however; they then worked together through purchase and litigation to acquire controlling patents in the gob feeder field. Ultimately, the entire industry took licences from the Hartford-Empire pool.

The operation of the Hartford-Empire pool was considerably different from the pool in *Standard Oil* discussed above. The Hartford-Empire licensees were subjected to a variety of restrictions as to field of use and output which gave the pool effective control of the glass container industry. The result, according to the district court, was "that invention of glassmaking machinery had been discouraged, that competition in the manufacture and sale or licensing of such machinery had been suppressed, and that the system of restricted licensing had been employed to suppress competition in the manufacture of unpatented glassware and to maintain prices of the manufactured product"[166]. The Supreme Court readily affirmed the district court's finding that these practices violated the Sherman Act, the bulk of the decision being given over to the appropriateness of various remedial provisions.

The recent Justice Department Guidelines express views on cross-licensing which echo the early decision in *Standard Oil* discussed above. Discussing the cross-licensing aspect of its hypothetical international exclusive cross-licensing case[167], the Department stated:

"In general, except in very highly concentrated markets involving homogeneous products, the cross-licensing of competing (or potentially competing) process patents alone is unlikely to be anticompetitive; rather, it generally is the restrictions that are used in connection with the cross-licensing that may raise antitrust concern. In fact, cross-licensing by itself is generally procompetitive because it expands access to

90

technology. In this case, for example, the cross-licence allows Alpha and Beta to use an alternative technology for producing X to which they otherwise would not have access. Similarly, if Alpha's and Beta's technologies are complementary (that is, if in at least some circumstances they are more efficient when used together), then the cross-license might enable Alpha and Beta to compete more effectively against the owners of other competing technologies. The cross-license may also allow Alpha and Beta to avoid protracted and expensive good-faith litigation over the validity and infringement of their respective patents. Assuming that the underlying transfer of technology in this case is not a sham, the Department would analyse its likely competitive effects using the rule-of-reason analysis set forth in Section 3.6 of these Guidelines."[168]

EEC

In the EEC, the patent licensing block exemption draws a sharp distinction between patent pools and cross-licences. Pools are simply excluded from all benefits of the block exemption under Article 5(1). Cross licences or know-how exchanges between horizontal competitors can, however, benefit from the regulation provided that the parties are not subject to any territorial restrictions within the common market on the "manufacture, use of putting on the market" of the licensed products or on the use of a licensed process [Article 5(2)]. The know-how regulation follows the same formula under its Articles 5(1)(1), (1)(3) and (2).

L.   REFUSAL TO LICENSE

One final category of conduct to be considered in this chapter is the refusal by a holder of an intellectual property right to license that right to others. Such cases have arisen in a variety of contexts, going beyond pure patent and know-how licensing, including copyrighted or otherwise protected industrial designs and protected plant varieties. Some of the jurisdictions discussed below reveal a marked shift in policy in this area since the 1974 OECD Report.

France

A 1985 opinion by the Competition Commission reviewed the practices of suppliers of *seeds for endive, corn and cereals*[169]. Apart from endive, these seeds were statutorily protected plant varieties benefiting from 20 to 25 years of protection.

Concerning the cereals sector, the Commission considered the practice of the varietal rights-holder to limit the number of licensees who reproduced and sold his protected seed variety and to organize his licensees into a "club".

The Commission found that the mere existence of plant variety clubs were legal under Article 50, although their activities might be examined. The legality of limited membership clubs followed from the fact that each club was organised by the holder of an exclusive right for the particular plant variety. The Commission reasoned that the principle of freedom of contract implied that consent to license that right could not be coerced. Hence the licensor could limit the number of licensees or refuse to grant any licences at all and reserve all production of the plant variety for himself.

The reasoning which the Commission applied here would not seem to be limited to protected plant varieties; the juxtaposition of freedom of contract and exclusive rights would seem to be applicable to industrial property rights generally. Thus one could read the *seeds* opinion as finding a general right for a holder of an industrial property right to refuse to license his invention.

United Kingdom

The issue of refusal to license intellectual property has come up three times in recent years in the UK, twice arising from OFT references to the Monopolies and Mergers Commission and once in private litigation. These cases touched upon a number of industrial property rights recognised in the UK, including patents, registered industrial designs and copyright.

A 1976 report by the MMC on the supply of *indirect electrostatic reprographic equipment*[170] examined the conduct of the Rank Xerox Co., a joint venture of Xerox Corp. and the Rank Organisation during a period when it held a near monopoly on the supply of plain paper photocopiers in the UK. Like Xerox in the US market, Rank Xerox's position was protected by numerous patents which it generally refused to license. The MMC report considered this conduct along with other potentially anticompetitive practices, including machine rentals aimed at price-discriminating between heavy and light users and other equipment leasing plans. While the Commission's response to these other issues are interesting, particularly its position on the consequences of price discrimination[171], the focus here is on its reaction to Rank Xerox's refusal to license its technology. The Commission found that Rank Xerox held over 1,000 UK patents on the indirect xerography process alone and that the sheer volume of patents impeded would-be competitors, given the expense in examining each patent. The Commission further found that this large patent portfolio coupled with Xerox's restrictive licensing policy served to maintain Xerox's dominant position in the UK. While not challenging the legality of Xerox's practices under the patent laws, the Commission found that the preservation of monopoly conditions thus produced were against the public interest. The Commission declined to issue a recommendation for compulsory licensing, however, given a consent order between Xerox and the US FTC which had recently issued. That order, as discussed below, required Xerox and Rank Xerox to license numerous patents.

Although the MMC did not recommend a patent licensing order in its report on Rank Xerox, it is clear that, at least as of 1977, the Commission can seek compulsory licensing to remedy a refusal to license in appropriate circumstances[172]. These remedies for refusing to license patents have no parallel however under British copyright law. The lack of such a remedy posed a dilemma for the MMC in 1985, in its report on *Ford*'s practice of refusing to license its copyrighted and registered designs for automotive body parts (crash and corrosion parts)[173].

In that investigation the MMC found that Ford's refusal to license its designs to aftermarket suppliers was both anticompetitive and not in the public interest. These conclusions were based on findings that competition from aftermarket suppliers was necessary to bring down Ford's prices for original equipment replacement parts. The Commission rejected Ford's arguments that competition in the new car market was a sufficient incentive for Ford to seek to keep repair costs low; most of the parts were purchased by subsequent owners and fleet buyers did not seem concerned about crash parts prices. Further, Ford only lowered its prices on these parts when aftermarket competition appeared, implying that competition at the new car level did not really influence parts prices. The Commission also gave little weight to Ford's argument that it needed the return on replacement parts to help defray the costs of designing new ones. Here the Commission expressed scepticism over the significance of the contribution given the magnitude of new car development costs and expressed the view that such costs were more appropriately borne in any event by new car buyers.

The Commission found that Ford's conduct was both anticompetitive and against the public interest, but found that it lacked an appropriate remedial tool. While the Commission could seek to get an order from the comptroller of patents for a compulsory licence in the case of a refusal to license a patented part, it lacked explicit authority to do so in the case of a design protected under copyright or registered design legislation. Finding no good remedy under existing law given Ford's unwillingness to license on reasonable terms (Ford was demanding royalties of 60 per cent), the Commission's report concluded with a recommendation that the laws establishing Ford's design protection be changed. In particular, the MMC recommended that both the Copyright Act and the Registered Designs Act be amended to limit the protection of body panel designs to a period of five years from the date of registration.

Ford's legal position changed markedly in the year following the MMC report, apparently leading it to give the Office of Fair Trading an undertaking to license its body parts at very modest royalties[174]. The change in Ford's fortunes followed from an opinion by the House of Lords in *British Leyland v. Armstrong Patents*[175]. In that case the Law Lords overturned an injunction issued against Armstrong restraining it from reproducing British Leyland designed exhaust systems and offering them in the aftermarket. While British Leyland had not refused to license its copyrighted and registered designs, indeed a number of firms had entered into agreements with British Leyland, Armstrong refused to accept a licence on British Leyland's terms and continued to manufacture exhaust system parts for British Leyland cars.

The judgement by Lord Templeman, joined in by a majority of the Law Lords, found that the copying of these parts did amount to an infringement of British Leyland's copyrights but overturned the injunction anyway. Noting that the case was highly significant in light of the expected movement by manufacturers to copyright their designs, and specifically noting the MMC's conclusion that similar conduct by Ford was anticompetitive, Lord Templeman looked to the common-law relationship between a grantor and a grantee and concluded that British Leyland, having sold a car, could not exercise its copyright to render that car unfit by preventing its repair. Thus, British Leyland's copyrights in its parts were rendered essentially unenforceable.

United States

Holders of patents in the United States have long been free to refuse unilaterally to license their property, although both the Federal Trade Commission and the Department of Justice brought actions in the early 1970s challenging that right. The principle was clearly expressed by the Supreme Court as early as 1902 in *Bement v. National Harrow Co*[176], where the Court emphasised that patent holders have "absolute freedom in the sale or use of their rights"[177]. Even if the patentee does not use the invention himself, he "has but suppressed his own" and the general public must simply rely on the self interest of the patentee to employ his invention[178].

Although the broad policy of *Bement* has never been overruled, one action by the Federal Trade Commission in 1973 challenged the patent licensing practice of Xerox Corporation[179], which then held substantial market power in plain paper copiers. One of the violations of Section 5 of the FTC Act alleged in the complaint was the practice of licensing patents only for coated paper and low-speed plain paper copiers, reserving for itself the market in high-speed plain paper copiers. The case, however, was settled in 1975. Thus the Commission's legal theories were never tested in a court of appeals. The settlement imposed obligations on Xerox and its foreign joint venturers (Fuji Film in Japan and the Rank Organisation in the UK) to license the patented technology and, at least in the United States, to license related know-how as well.

Subsequently, a private plaintiff also challenged Xerox's patent acquisition and licensing practices in *SCM Corp. v. Xerox Corp*[180]. SCM alleged in that case that Xerox's acquisition of patents and later refusal to license them violated sections 1 and 2 of the Sherman Act and section 7 of the Clayton Act. On appeal from a jury verdict in favour of SCM, the court of appeals ruled that the jury's grant of monetary damages to SCM was improper, as Xerox's refusal to license lawfully acquired patents "cannot trigger any liability under the antitrust laws"[181]. In reaching this conclusion the court of appeals examined and rejected SCM's analogy to other refusals to deal by a monopolist. Here, the defendant was merely enforcing rights given to him under the patent laws. Further, the defendant was engaged in unilateral conduct; while a concerted refusal to license could indeed provide a basis for liability, unilateral conduct could not[182].

Within months of the decision in *SCM v. Xerox*, the Court of Appeals for the Ninth Circuit came to a similar conclusion in *United States v. Westinghouse*[183], which involved a civil action brought by the Justice Department in 1970 against Westinghouse for its policy of granting to Mitsubishi Heavy Industries only licences on its foreign patents. While the licences which Westinghouse did grant helped Mitsubishi to grow into a significant competitor in electrical equipment, Westinghouse's refusal to license its Canadian and American patents prevented Mitsubishi from entering those markets.

The court of appeals rejected the government's theory that Westinghouse, having made Mitsubishi dependent on its technology and thus unable to enter North America without licences, was under an obligation to license the potential competitor it had helped to create. The court of appeals found that because Westinghouse was doing no more than seeking to protect its rewards under the patent laws, it was under no duty to license the North American patents. Indeed, it agreed with the trial court that the government's theory was aimed at narrowing the scope of patent protection, a choice, the court suggested, best left to the legislature.

One final case which could be considered here is the FTC's 1980 decision in *Dupont*[184], a decision which shows the movement of the agency's position from the *Xerox* matter. In *Dupont*, the Commission had charged that the company had attempted to monopolize the market for titanium dioxide pigments (TiO2). At the time, TiO2 could be produced by any of three combinations of processes and raw materials. Dupont alone had developed and commercialised one of these technologies in the early 1950s but the other two technologies remained competitive until the early 1970s, when shifting raw materials prices and the impact of pollution control costs gave the Dupont process a decisive cost advantage. Dupont refused to license its know-how and, by aggressively adding capacity, discouraged its competitors from building the large-scale new plants necessary to learn the secrets of Dupont's technology.

Following an administrative trial and an appeal to the Commission, the Commissioners concluded that Dupont's conduct was not unreasonable and dismissed the complaint. With respect to Dupont's refusal to license its know-how, the Commission held that

"in the context of this case, we can find no basis for concluding that Dupont's refusal to license its technology, whether taken separately or together with the other conduct, was unjustified. There is no evidence, for example, that respondent used unreasonable means to acquire its know-how, or that it joined with others in preventing access by competitors. Complaint counsel cite no authority for the proposition that Dupont should have licensed its technology, and we are aware of none. Whatever may be the proper result in other factual settings, we are not persuaded that the refusal to license in this situation provides a basis for liability; in fact, imposition of a duty to license might serve to chill the very kind of innovative process that led to Dupont's cost advantage."[185]

EEC

A recent decision by the Court of Justice considered whether a refusal to license could be considered to be an abuse of dominant position under Article 86. In that case, *Volvo/Veng*[186], the Court took up questions referred by the High Court of England and Wales in a case arising out of Weng's importation into the United Kingdom of replacement automobile fenders which infringed Volvo's registered designs. Among the questions submitted to the Court of Justice were whether the possession of an exclusive right, in itself, established a dominant position for purposes of Article 86 and whether the refusal to license an exclusive right could establish a presumption that the dominant position was abused.

The Court of Justice dealt only indirectly with the first question, focusing instead on what could constitute an abuse. Here the Court was clear that refusing to license, taken alone, could not be considered to be an abuse, given that the very nature of intellectual property rights was the power to exclude others from copying. The Court went on, however, to find that the *exercise* of the exclusive right could be regulated under Article 86, thus following the existence/exercise distinction set out in the *Centrafarm* decision discussed previously. According to the Court, a violation of Article 86 could be found in the context of automobile parts in such actions as the refusal to supply independent repair shops, setting prices at an unfair level or in stopping production of a part needed for a model still in use in significant numbers.

Concerning the presumption of dominance from the existence of an exclusive right, the Court stated that it was not reaching that issue but its discussion implied nonetheless that dominance would have to be established case-by-case rather than merely assumed. In particular, the Court held that the practices described above could be abusive when employed by dominant firms, implying that some holders of exclusive rights would not be considered to be dominant. Unfortunately, the opinion gave no guidance as to how dominance should be established in various situations. In the case of automobile parts, one could readily find, as the MMC did in the *Ford* matter discussed above, that the manufacturer enjoyed substantial power in the parts market if it could exclude competitors. Thus, while the Court's decision in *Volvo* holds out the possibility that market power may not be found in future cases, the English court handling the case may well, following *Ford*, find market power to be present here and then go on to examine Volvo's conduct.

M. DISCUSSION

At this point it may be useful to look at the cases just presented from the point of view of the economic criteria identified in Chapter 3. In that chapter a number of possibly pro- and anticompetitive effects of licensing agreements were set out. Further, two particular articles of faith in the patent licensing area were questioned: that the exclusive rights of a patent grant provide market power and that patent licensing can leverage or extend whatever market power does exist.

The notion of market power provides a good starting point. In Chapter 3 it was argued that the grant of patent rights does not necessarily produce any market power in the patentee because many patents are not marketable inventions and most of those which are face competition from other products. Thus, a case-by-case inquiry into the market power question was said to be appropriate. The cases just reviewed, however, generally take market power as a given fact in the patent context, provoking concern over patent licensing practices which may have no basis in fact.

Many of the decisions in the United States, for example, presumed market power because a patent was involved, leading to per se illegality of practices which may or may not harm competition. The presumption continues to this day under the majority opinion in *Jefferson Parish*, but the minority opinion in that case indicates that the presumption may be eliminated in the US. In the EC, the presumption of market power is also present even though the cases do not discuss it as such. It can be seen in the concern expressed both by the Commission and the Court of Justice in preserving intrabrand competition, which is of concern more when substitute goods are lacking than when they are present. In *Maize Seed*, for example, the Court of Justice did not consider competition from other varieties of maize seed and focused on preserving intrabrand competition by protecting parallel imports. There is some recent movement in the EC, however, similar to what seems to be occurring in the US. In *Interpane/Boussois*, the Commission still discussed preserving intrabrand competition but did examine the existence of other glass coating technologies and the competition they provided. In the recent *Volvo/Veng* decision, the Court has also hinted that market power may not always be found. Other decisions giving some recognition to interbrand competition include *Sodastream* (competition from traditional soft-drink suppliers) and *Agricultural Chemicals* (discussing competing lines and actual anticompetitive effects product by product). These latter decisions are useful in showing how a realistic appraisal of market power can reveal that an otherwise potentially objectionable practice may be harmless under the facts, e.g., the *Sodastream* tie-in given other sources of soft drinks.

The leveraging of market power is another concept which survives in many cases, particularly in the US. Many of those cases make no effort to determine the economic basis of a transaction and misidentify the appropriation of the surplus generated by the innovation as leveraging, resulting in an ill-considered condemnation of a licensing arrangement. This is seen most clearly in such tie-in cases as *B.B. Chemical* and *Mercoid* and in packaging licensing cases such as *American Securit* and *Zenith Radio*. The EC, too, has not been immune to the concept of leveraging, as shown by the opinion in *Vaessen/Morris*, which was concerned over an extension of monopoly to the sausage casing market, and by its restrictive treatment of tie-ins in the block exemptions.

These cases cited in the preceding paragraph share more than an affinity for the monopoly extension theory; in each there is an absence of market definition and analysis of how the market power created by the patent could be extended. In *Mercoid*, for example, there is no discussion of competing home heating designs or how the taking of profits on unpatented controls in any way threatened competition in the control market. The reader does not learn from the decision the structure of the control market and how Honeywell's tie-in affected it. Likewise, in *Vaessen/Morris*, we have no idea how Morris' casing tie-in threatened competition in the casing market. Perhaps the only opinion to reason clearly on extension (apart from the recent dissent in *Jefferson Parish*) was the early decision in *A.B. Dick*, where the Court held that it was not cause for concern that the patentee chose to take his profits on ink instead of his patented machine, competition in the ink market being hardly threatened by the tie-in.

A very different set of assumptions is apparent in the recently published US DOJ Guidelines, which do not assume that patents necessarily create market power. Moreover, the Guidelines are not hostile to market power when it is created through innovation. Thus the Guidelines distinguish between the permissible capturing of a surplus created by innovative effort and impermissible efforts to create market power through licensing agreements. In this latter area the Guidelines do not adopt any mechanical notion of monopoly extension or leveraging but set out a method for case-by-case analysis of possible pro-and anticompetitive effects. The assumptions and analysis set out in Guidelines represents the method by which the DOJ will review cases and may well influence courts in the future, but private litigants will still operate under the broad lines of the decisions set out in this chapter.

While a number of the cases have shown a tendency to cling to some questionable concepts, others show why licensing abuses can create serious competitive problems. Cartelization emerged as a real problem in a variety of contexts. The creation of an industry-standard around a protected design, for example, was part of an effort to cartelize the French beverage case industry. Cartelization through the licensing of all competitors under a weak patent combined with restraints which went well beyond the legitimate needs of the patentee (setting high minimum prices on competing unpatented products) was part of an effort to cartelize the US wallboard industry in *US Gypsum*. Patent pooling likewise was a tool in efforts to organize the US market in glass containers (*Hartford-Empire*). Note, however, that pooling alone does not imply cartel activity. It can, for example, be a legitimate method to resolve infringement litigation, as in *Standard Oil*, or to gain the use of an improvement patent held by another, as in *Line Material*, although the Court condemned the pool (wrongly, it seems) in *Line Material*. A further complication is that some of the justification offered for pooling may be spurious, covering an effort at cartelization, as in the seemingly trumped-up infringement litigation in *Hartford-Empire*.

A major question for competition authorities to resolve, then, is whether a particular licensing agreement or pool is directed at the suppression of competition between the patentee(s) and competing firms. If that is the case, many of the clauses reviewed in this chapter, e.g. restraints on prices, output, territories or fields of use, could well represent the implementation of a cartel agreement. On the other hand, if the restraints are directed vertically, the competitive effects are likely to be completely different and pose little cause for concern.

Vertical restraints can be used, for example, to give the licensee sufficient local market power to have an incentive to invest in the production or promotion of the innovation. This may be brought about by granting an exclusive territory, e.g. as in *Interpane/Boussois*, *Maize Seed*, *Kabelmetal/Luchaire* and *GTE/Sylvania*. As recognised by the Court in *GTE/Sylvania* and by the DOJ in its Guidelines, the use of such restraints may promote interbrand competition by inducing the local licensee to invest in capital and labour, to engage in promotional activities and to provide a high level of service and repair through the avoidance of free-rider effects.

Vertical restraints on price and output are closely related in economic effect to territorial restraints. Maintaining a certain price level, for example, can provide the local licensee with rents which, in the face of interbrand competition, might fuel local interbrand competition in promotion and service. The cases, however, generally do not recognize this pro-competitive aspect of vertical price and output restraints, and are often hostile to both types of restraints, as in *Yakult*, *Bremsrollen*, the EC block exemptions and the Japanese guidelines (at least with respect to price terms). On the other hand, the US Supreme Court does now credit the pro-competitive aspects of all vertical restraints, as seen in the recent resale price case *Sharp Electronics*, the reasoning of which seems fully applicable to the intellectual property context, and that view is followed in the new DOJ Guidelines. In this context, efforts to protect each territory from parallel imports could be argued to be aimed at preserving the licensee's incentive to invest in and promote the new technology.

Another pro-competitive effect of vertical restraints can be seen in the aid they give to the licensor to engage in output-expanding price-discrimination, an effect recognised by the dissenting justices in *Jefferson Parish* and by the MMC in *Xerox*. This can be accomplished, for example, by setting different prices in different territories or fields of use, or through the use of metering tie-ins. The cases, however, (with the exception of *Jefferson Parish*) make little or no mention of the benefits of such practices. While a metering tie-in was permitted in *A.B. Dick*, the US Supreme Court condemned the practice in such later cases as *Motion Picture Patents*, *BB Chemical* and the various *Salt* cases. Likewise, the EC Commission has shown little appreciation of this aspect in its condemnation of tie-ins in *Vaessen/Morris* and the block exemptions, limiting the use of tie-ins to cases where technical or quality control reasons require them. The new Japanese guidelines take a similar approach to the EC on tie-ins.

Price discrimination by a licensor receives a favourable reception, however, when it can be accomplished through a field-of-use restriction. Thus, the EC block exemptions and the Japanese guidelines, both hostile to tie-ins, approve field-of-use restrictions. Similarly, field-of-use restrictions have been permitted in the US in cases such as *General Talking Pictures* and *Studiengesellschaft Kohle*. The latter case, moreover, intuitively focused on the key question in examining the effect of the restraint: whether output was increased by the restricted licence. This recognition of the output-enhancing potential of a price discriminating restraint is rare in the cases.

The cases also show themselves to be fairly insensitive to the function of certain clauses in lowering transaction costs and risk and thereby raising returns to licensors. Thus package licensing arrangements are generally condemned where they involve "forcing", as under the EC regulations or under such US cases as *American Securit* or *Zenith Radio*, even though such techniques, designed to help the licensor appropriate his surplus more efficiently, are hardly likely to be welcomed by licensees. Likewise, the decision in the German *Windsurfing* decision found a royalty based on the price of the final product to be an unlawful extension of the sail-rig monopoly when that royalty mechanism seems instead to have been an efficient way to solve a problem in bargaining over the rig licence. That is, when bargaining neither party could likely foresee the contours of the product market, including price levels and the ultimate product mix, and thus would not know in advance what value to put on the rig licence. That value, however, would be known after-the-fact by sales figures, thus making royalties on total sales a useful device. The Japanese guidelines may also limit the use of royalty terms to solve certain problems in contracting by stating that charging royalties on products or services other than the patented goods may be found to be unfair. Such clauses may be useful, however, in eliminating policing costs and ensuring optimal input mix or exclusivity.

Another problem relates to the focus found in many of the cases on intrabrand competition. By not focusing on the economic uses and procompetitive effects on interbrand competition of the various vertical restraints, difficult burdens are placed on licensors and inconsistent policies are created. Numerous decisions, for example, have equated the "restriction" on trade inherent in a vertical restraint, e.g. the grant of an exclusive licence, with anticompetitive conduct when such a restriction is likely to *promote* interbrand competition. Many of the decisions have gone on to assume that the thus-defined restrictive agreement was unlawful unless it could be justified in some way. Justifications have been found generally in either of two ways: (1) the restriction was expressly permitted under patent law or (2) the restriction could be shown to be "indispensible" for technical progress. The latter test may pose a heavy burden on a licensor who at the time of licensing has no way to guarantee the success of the licensing arrangement. The former test may lead to results where clauses having similar economic effects are judged differently. For example, restrictions aimed at increasing potential licensee profits and thus giving the licensee an incentive to invest in and promote a new technology are often permitted if done in the form of exclusive territories or field-of-use restraints, restraints which are often recognized as permissible under patent law, but prohibited if done by price or output restraints, the latter restraints often being subject to per se prohibition under competition law. Likewise, efforts to expand output and maximize profits by charging light users less is generally permitted if it can be done by a field-of-use restriction but prohibited if done by a metering tie-in. Efforts should be made to give coherent treatment to the various possible types of clauses, beginning with a clear understanding of the pro- and anticompetitive issues involved, and by focusing from the outset on interbrand competition and the likely effects of the licensing agreement on competition at that level.

In conclusion, this review of cases shows a need to refocus somewhat competition policy concerns over licensing practices. Practices aimed at restraining horizontal competition should remain, as before, a matter of vigilance. Where, however, the restraints operate in a vertical fashion, a considerably different analysis may be appropriate. Here, practices which help the licensor increase the output of his innovation (and likely raise his returns simultaneously) could be recognized as pro-competitive, even if the surplus appears to be gathered on another product. Likewise, vertical restraints which promote interbrand competition by encouraging the local licensee to invest in and promote the innovation and by protecting that licensee from free riders could also be seen as pro-competitive. The risks to competition posed by such practices are real but may be narrow in scope, and require careful examination of the market(s) involved, as suggested in Chapter 3.

Chapter 6

CONCLUSIONS

This report has reviewed the application of competition policy to certain intellectual property licensing agreements. The analysis has focused primarily on patent and know-how licensing agreements but has also included cases touching on protected industrial designs and plant varieties. Thus the scope of the report and these conclusions do not extend to areas of protected artistic expression such as copyright. Trademark and franchising matters also were not considered. Likewise, the report does not reach competition policy issues outside the intellectual property area.

The inspiration for this report was the sense that the Committee's previous work in this area, the 1972 Report on Restrictive Practices Relating to Patents and Licences and the related 1974 Council Recommendation, might need revision in light of intervening developments in legal and economic thinking. That concern was borne out, as the previous chapters attest, leading the Committee to outline here an approach to the analysis of intellectual property licensing practices better attuned to the various possible pro- and anticompetitive effects of such agreements.

The approach of this report is both general and forward-looking. That is, the report presents a method of analysis which does not take account of existing statutory structures or countervailing policy considerations. For example, some of the licensing restrictions discussed below are per se unlawful in various member countries, yet this report suggests that a case-by-case treatment would be more appropriate. Given that competition policy officials are bound to enforce existing law, the analysis presented here should be seen as an analytical framework for policy development.

This report argues that long-standing notions about conflict between intellectual property rights and competition policy should be reconsidered. Intellectual property rights, like rights in other forms of property, are necessary for the functioning of a competitive, market-based economy. The earning of profits through the exploitation of intellectual property rights either by the innovator himself or by others through licensing is both the reward for innovative effort and a tangible incentive to others to undertake R & D efforts. Thus, the ability of the innovator to capture the surplus generated by his innovation benefits competition in the long run by encouraging others to innovate as well.

The innovator's use of his exclusive rights to capture parts of what would otherwise be consumer surplus does impose costs however. In particular, the exercise of exclusive rights produces in the short run a less-than-optimal use of the innovation, that is, it can result in the pricing of intellectual property greater than its marginal cost, which is zero. This short-run misallocation is the price that has to be paid to secure an improved long-term dynamic resource efficiency through an optimal level of innovative activity. Otherwise, it is unlikely that profits from innovative activities will be sufficient to keep such activities at an optimal long-term level. This would be detrimental to the long-term interests of consumers.

The short-run misallocations may, however, be reduced by certain licensing techniques which operate merely to help the licensor to capture the surplus inherent in the innovation and could also contribute to the dissemination and utilization of the innovation. The appropriation of the normal consumer surplus through the licensing of an innovation should not be confused with other efforts to capture consumer surplus through cartel activity, eg., through a sham licensing agreement. This report draws a fundamental distinction between the competitive effects and thus the legality of these two types of activity.

The belief that permitting innovators to capture the full returns inherent in their innovations leads to a long-term efficient use of resources, thus benefiting consumers, is basic to the analysis of this report. If one believed that less than full returns to innovators would result in the same level of innovative activity in the economy, or at least would generate "enough" new products and processes, one would view differently the economic effects of innovators capturing their full returns. From that point of view, one might prefer to see innovations distributed widely and inexpensively throughout the economy. However, one cannot well judge either how much innovation is sufficient for economic efficiency or how much incentive is needed to bring it forth. Thus this report favours permitting an innovator to capture the surplus inherent in the innovation as the safest course for ensuring competition and growth in the long run.

Diverse national situations may, however, cause a government to restrain the innovator's ability to capture his rents. One case is that of a country which does not permit licensors to maximise their returns because the country is a net importer of technology. Domestic distributional effects might also lead a country to a different policy balance than that suggested here. Some countries view prohibiting certain kinds of agreements as a way to protect licensees' freedom of action or to serve certain goals of fairness to licensees. Finally, some countries believe that certain licence restrictions, such as exclusive grant-backs, reduce the incentive of licensees to innovate. Thus, they believe legal limitations on those restrictions are necessary to ensure a better balance between the licensee's and the licensor's incentives to innovate, which these countries believe is fundamental to higher levels of innovative activity in their economies.

Competition policy cases involving intellectual property licensing have often been based on the presumption that the holder of an intellectual property right automatically had market power based on that right. The granting of a patent, however, has no necessary relationship with market power. Even where the patent relates to a commercially viable product or process, that product will likely face alternative technologies in the market place, limiting its market power. Thus, to the extent that the competitive effects of an intellectual property licensing agreement turns on the market power of the property, competition policy authorities need to review carefully the market situation of the property rather than merely to assume that market power exists. Such an analysis would include both an inventory of competing technologies to produce a given product as well as an assessment of substitute products. Where a technology lacks market power, restrictions in the licensing agreement may well be procompetive, in the absence of horizontal restraints discussed below. Even where a technology with market power is licensed, vertical restraints in that licence agreement may still be procompetitive in the absence of certain market conditions, also discussed more fully below.

Another aspect of many competition decisions reviewed in this report is the concern that the holder of an intellectual property right with market power would be able to leverage or extend that market power through restrictions in licensing agreements. Many of these decisions, however, do not distinguish between two distinct ways in which licensing restrictions can raise returns to the licensor. Restrictions which operate merely to help the licensor capture the surplus inherent in the innovation should not be seen as anticompetitive. In certain circumstances, however, the same kinds of restrictions which generally promote competition may operate to increase the market power of the licensor. The task for competition policy officials in reviewing licensing agreements is to identify this latter effect without blocking possibly procompetitive agreements.

The risk that a licensing agreement will operate to increase the market power of the licensor beyond that inherent in the innovation differs between horizontal and vertical agreements. Horizontal agreements, agreements between actual or potential competitors in a given market, can pose considerable risks that the result will be an increase in market power through cartelization. This cartelization might result directly from the operation of the agreement, for example from restrictions relating to price, output, territories, fields of use or customers, or indirectly in the case of restrictions which facilitate tacit collusion or the implementation of a separate cartel understanding. Licensing agreements which operate in this manner and are not reasonably related to a transfer of technology are appropriately treated in the same fashion as other cartel agreements between actual or potential competitors. This question of whether an agreement reasonably relates to a transfer of technology can be difficult and becomes more so when the transfer involves non-public know-how. This is one area where there is a significant difference, at least for competition authorities, between patent and know-how licensing agreements.

Many horizontal licensing agreements will not fall within the above category. For horizontal agreements which do show a reasonable link to a transfer of technology, it cannot be presumed that the agreement has either an anticompetitive aim or effect. For example, some licensing agreements between horizontal competitors may be created to settle disputes over conflicting or blocking patents. In such situations, cross-licensing agreements may serve as an efficient dispute settlement mechanism which operates procompetitively by increasing the diffusion of technology. Moreover, in certain cases, restrictive clauses in licensing agreements between competitors can enhance technology transfers and thus be procompetitive. Thus, competition officials need to determine the likely competitive effect of each horizontal agreement.

One way to estimate the potential anticompetitive effect of a restrictive licensing agreement between horizontal competitors is to assess the market shares of the firms involved. For example, if the restriction involved two fringe firms, the loss of competition between those two firms could be de minimis or even outweighed by the creation of a more efficient competitor. Assessing the market share of a technology poses particular problems, however, as current market share figures may not reveal the future significance of a technology. Thus competition authorities need to be prepared to evaluate both the present and likely future commercial importance of each firm's technology. Assuming that a significant market share will be covered by the agreement, competition authorities will then need to assess the risk of cartelization against possible pro-competitive effects from the restraints which are described below.

In some cases the distinction between a horizontal and vertical agreement may be difficult to make. For example, an agreement licensing technology to a foreign producer of the same product will require a careful analysis of whether that firm is a competitively significant potential competitor in the domestic market. If the foreign firm is such a significant potential competitor, the licensing restrictions should be considered to be horizontal. On the other hand, licensing technology to a firm which is not a potential competitor in the domestic market would be more appropriately viewed as vertical in nature — the sale of an input to a downstream firm.

Another difficulty is in separating vertical restraints which are the implementation of a cartel agreement from vertical restraints which are established by the independent actions of licensors. An example of a vertical restraint which implements a horizontal agreement could be two licensors which conspire to fix *price* at the licensee level. Ostensibly competing licensees could likewise conspire to fix prices between them by having price restrictive clauses imposed upon them by their respective licensors. Such arrangements, which could also involve, e.g. *output*, *territorial*, *customer* or *field-of-use* restraints, are appropriately seen as horizontal restraints and treated as such, even though the implementing mechanism is through vertical licensing arrangements.

A different situation is presented where a licensor acts independently to impose price, output, territorial or customer restraints on its licensee(s). Here the restraints are purely vertical as they do not result from a cartel agreement but nonetheless may pose the risk of significant anticompetitive effects. In particular, the implementation of vertical price, output, customer or territorial restraints may promote tacit collusion at either the licensor or licensee level.

In this context, *exclusivity* clauses can be used anticompetitively to exclude competing licensors. Exclusivity in distribution can deny a distribution network to a competing licensed product, potentially raising barriers to entry if the competitor then faces slow or costly entry at the distribution level. Exclusivity in the use of a technology can likewise foreclose technology markets to competing licensors and may reduce the incentive to engage in efforts to develop competing technologies. Exclusive *grantback* clauses can similarly work to reduce the incentives to a licensee to develop a competing technology. They also can maintain or increase the market power of the licensor.

Tie-in clauses can also be used anticompetitively in cases where the licensor can use such a restraint to gain a dominant position in the market for the second, tied good. A dominant position in the tied good could in itself be a source of rents and could also raise barriers to entry in the market for the tying good, if the former good were necessary for consumption of the latter.

Pooling and *cross-licensing* agreements can be anticompetitive through a combination of vertical and horizontal effects, apart from the obvious risks of cartelization posed by such agreements. In particular, such agreements may lead to a standardization of products at either the licensor or licensee level, which could facilitate tacit collusion or the implementation of a separate cartel understanding.

Finally, a *no challenge* clause may be considered to be anticompetitive even if it operates to make the licensor more likely to engage in licensing activities. Here, the promotion of licensing is subordinated to the overriding interest of some governments in assuring that rights in patents are held only by those who have earned them. Limitations on no challenge clauses may be appropriate to ensure that licensees, the parties with both the technical ability and economic incentive to challenge improperly granted patents, remain free to do so.

The possible anticompetitive effects of vertical restraints outlined above are well known. What has received less attention is the market conditions necessary for these effects to be realized as well as possible pro-competitive effects from the same restraints in other circumstances.

Anticompetitive effects on consumers from vertical restraints are likely to arise only under a limited set of market conditions. The first is a high degree of concentration in the market at the licensor level, with the larger licensors using the same or similar restraints. Second, a large proportion of the licensee market must be subject to the restraint. Finally, entry in the restrained market must be difficult. If one of these conditions is absent, the vertical restraint is not likely to affect consumers anticompetitively, as either co-ordination among licensors will break down, the unrestrained portion of the licensee market will grow, or new entry will occur or at least threaten in that market. Thus, in the example of the price, output, customer or territorial restraints discussed above, the presence of an unrestrained firm at either the licensor or licensee level could grow at the expense of the restrained firms. In the tie-in example, an alternative source of the tied good would restrain the ability of the tying firm to exploit its position in the tied good market. In the case of exclusivity, the ability of a competing licensor to find or create licensees would limit the licensor's power over price.

Market structure and entry conditions are crucial as those factors vary significantly across OECD countries. Thus, for example, a vertical restraint by a given licensor in a smaller, more concentrated or more entry-constrained market might pose a considerably higher risk of anticompetitive effects than the same restraint by the same licensor in a larger or more open national market.

The various ways in which a vertical agreement can promote competition were not discussed in this Committee's 1972 Report and indeed only recently have been recognised. Thus it is useful to provide some examples of the principal possible procompetitive effects of different types of clauses which have been examined in this report.

Territorial restraints can be used to preserve margins of both the licensor and the licensee by limiting intrabrand competition within a given territory, in order to induce investment in the use and promotion of new technology. Territorial restraints can also help the establishment of different prices in different markets in response to local demand functions. This result is procompetitive in that it results in a lower price where consumers have a higher cross-elasticity of demand, resulting in higher overall output than if the licensor were limited to a single monopoly price across all territories.

Exclusivity agreements can have similar effects as the territorial restrictions discussed above. That is, a licensee granted exclusivity in its territory is more likely to invest in promoting the licensed technology than one faced with the threat of potential intrabrand competition in its market. From the point of view of the licensor, a commitment by the licensee to deal exclusively in the technology of the licensor provides assurance that the licensee will devote its best efforts to the promotion of the licensor's technology.

Price agreements can guarantee margins to licensees, in order to induce investment in the production and promotion of new technology. This effect at the licensee level can serve to promote interbrand competition. Such agreements can also preserve returns to the licensor, increasing the returns to innovation and the incentives both to innovate and to license.

Output restraints can be viewed in the same way as price restraints. Such restraints can be used to preserve licensee margins and thus the licensee's incentive to promote the new technology. Output restraints can also be used to preserve the licensor's profits, especially where it too produces in the same market. Thus, a holder of an intellectual property right may increase total output through licensing another firm even if it limits that firm's output.

Field-of-use restrictions can help implement and reinforce a number of the functions of the restraints set out above. Licensing according to field of use can help the licensor create an exclusive licensee in each of several fields of use, increasing the number of licensees while preserving the incentive for each licensee to promote the technology within its field-of-use. Such restraints can thus work to increase the diffusion of the technology. Further, field-of-use restraints can work in conjunction with other restraints to permit a licensor to decrease price and increase output in a particular field of use.

Tie-ins can be used to increase output by permitting the licensor to charge according to intensity of use, allowing him to charge lower prices to light users. This metering function can also help to disseminate new technology by permitting firms with incomplete information about the value of a new technlogy to try that technology at lower risk than if the licensor had to charge a single monopoly price. Other functions of tie-ins include maintaining the quality of the final product by assuring the quality of various inputs and maintaining licensee productive efficiency by controlling the proportions of substitutable inputs.

Package licensing can promote licensing activities by reducing transaction costs between licensor and licensee, raising returns to the licensor for a given number of transactions or permitting more transactions at constant returns.

Royalty terms can be used to promote the efficiency of a licensing transaction in a variety of ways. For example, a term requiring the licensor to pay royalties on total output can be used to avoid policing efforts or the risk of litigation to determine how much of which technology was used in the production of a final product, as well as to leave the licensee with an incentive to choose the most efficient mix of inputs.

Grantback clauses make it less risky for a firm to license its technology by assuring it the use of any improvements discovered by the licensee. Grantbacks particularly lack the potential for anticompetitive effects when they are reciprocal or non-exclusive.

Pooling and cross-licensing can be used as an efficient method of resolving disputes involving conflicting patent claims or blocking patents. Also, these agreements, by leading to a standardization of products, can lead to increased compatibility between products and thus increase competition.

The discussion above gives some examples of how restrictive clauses in patent licensing agreements can promote increased returns to the licensor, increased interbrand competition and the wider dissemination of a new technology.

There does not appear to be any reason to treat know-how licensing agreements more restrictively than agreements involving legally protected intellectual property, apart from the difficulty alluded to earlier in detecting sham agreements involving know-how. There do appear, however, to be reasons to treat know-how agreements more liberally given certain aspects of the nature of know-how. In particular, since know-how enjoys less protection than patents, significant weight should be given to restraints reasonably related to preserving secrecy. Likewise, the need to prevent post-agreement exploitation should be recognized, as know-how, once transferred, cannot be recalled.

The report has dealt with the question of compulsory licensing only indirectly. While the legitimate interest of a nation to order compulsory licensing in appropriate circumstances cannot be doubted, it should be recognized that such licences are rarely granted in practice. Moreover, a number of the potentially procompetitive effects set out above stem from the licensor's ability to limit the firms permitted to deal in the new technology. Thus, as far as competition policy is concerned, the licensor should generally be free to *refuse to license* other firms and to limit exploitation of the innovation either to itself or to its selected licensee(s).

This discussion of the various possible effects from restrictive clauses in licensing agreements shows that, for practically every type of clause considered here, the restraint may operate either to promote or reduce competition, depending on the circumstances. Thus, leaving aside horizontal agreements where the restraints bear no reasonable relationship to the licensed technology, competition officials should review licensing agreements on a case-by-case basis. When assessing the likely effects of vertically restrictive agreements, efforts should be made to give coherent treatment to the various possible types of clauses. That is, clauses with similar purposes or likely effects should be given similar treatment as far as possible.

This report suggests that competition authorities should review licensing agreements on a case-by-case basis. In order to increase predictability of the outcome of such reviews, competition authorities should consider preparing guidelines to clarify as much as possible the criteria applicable to licensing agreements under competition laws. In addition, procedures for speedy review of licensing agreements are desirable.

The views set out above reflect developments in the analysis of certain aspects of vertical restraints in general and patent licensing agreements in particular which have blossomed in the years following the 1972 report and the 1974 Council Recommendation on Restrictive Business Practices in Patent Licensing. Thus, there is considerable divergence between these conclusions and that Recommendation. Given the adoption of these conclusions, the Council withdrew the 1974 Recommendation on 31st March 1989 and recommended that governments take into account to the extent possible under existing law the analysis presented in this report.

NOTES AND REFERENCES

Chapter 1

1. See, e.g., M.J. Meurer, *An Economic Analysis of Royalty Terms in Patent Licences*, 67 Minnesota L. Rev. 1198 note 3 (1983) (Scientific and technical advance accounted for 48 per cent of the rise in output per worker between 1929 and 1969, citing E. Denison, *Accounting for United States Economic Growth*, 1929-1969 at 131-37 (1974); F.M. Scherer, *Innovation and Growth*, 257-69 (1984); J. Schmookler, *Invention and Economic Growth*, 196 (1966).

2. Kamien and Schwartz outline a complex interaction between market structure and innovation. They find the greatest level of innovation in markets where there is some opportunity for realizing monopoly profits from innovation and in markets where an innovator can erode the market share of incumbent firms. Broad generalizations are risky, however, as factors such as technological opportunity can vary across sectors. Further, concentration can be affected by innovation as well as vice versa. M.I. Kamien and N.L. Schwartz, *Market Structure and Innovation*, 95, 218-19 (1982). See also, D.H. Ginsburg, *Antitrust, Uncertainty and Technological Innovation*, 24 Antitrust Bulletin 635, 636.

3. *Competition Policy and Joint Ventures*, paras. 58, 317, OECD (1986).

4. Recommendation of the Council Concerning Action Against Restrictive Business Practices Relating to the Use of Patents and Licences.

5. One survey of firms' licensing practices found that the great majority of firms licensed know-how with their patents. Pure know-how licences were much less frequently used and pure patent licences were still less frequent. F.J. Contractor, *Technology Licensing Practice in US Companies: Corporate and Public Policy Implications*, Columbia Journal of World Business 80, 84 (Fall 1983).

Chapter 2

1. See e.g., *Intellectual Property Rights and Innovation*, 6-7 (Cmnd. 9117, 1983); M.I. Kamien and N.L. Schwartz, *Market Structure and Innovation*, 8, 100-01 (1982).

2. *Intellectual Property Rights*, supra note 1. One survey of licensors in the United States found that licensing income had "grown in strategic importance in recent years. The reason cited most frequently for licensing programmes was to gain royalties over time, followed by new market development. F.J. Contractor, *Technology Licensing Practices in US Companies: Corporate and Public Policy Implications*, Columbia Journal of World Business; 80 and Table 8 (Fall 1983).

3. See, e.g., *Concentration and Competition Policy*, Paras. 11-12, OECD (1979); J.A. Ordover, *Economic Foundations and Considerations in Protecting Industrial and Intellectual Property*, 53 Antitrust L.J. 503, 510-11 (1984).

4. Ordover, supra note 3 at 505; F.M. Scherer, *Innovation and Growth*, 257-63 (1984).

5. J. Schmookler, *Invention and Economic Growth*, 206 (1966); F. Machlup, *The Production and Distribution of Knowledge in the United States* at 175 (1962).

6. Perhaps the most extensive group of case studies were performed by J. Schmookler, who compared patent statistics with investment trends and other economic indicators in a variety of industries and in a variety of technologies within a given industry. Schmookler, supra note 5. He found that capital goods inventions tended to vary over time "directly with and in response to sales of capital goods in that field". Id. at 162.

   Later work nuanced Schmookler's findings in an important respect. "Demand pull" is better seen as a necessary but not sufficient condition for innovation to occur; there must also be a technological opportunity. Thus one can conceptualize supply ("technological push") and demand ("demand pull") curves for innovation. Shifting, either curve will affect the level of innovation brought forth. Rosenberg, *Inside the Black Box: Technology and Economics*, 228-32 (1982).

   Following an extensive review of the literature, Kamien and Schwartz summarized the interaction as follows: "At present, the conventional wisdom appears to be that demand pull or economic opportunity is more important than technological opportunity as a spur to invention. It is difficult to argue that the opportunity to profit creates no incentive to invent. This knowledge, however, does not go very far in indicating when, and even if, an invention will be forthcoming. Perhaps the most important insight emerging from this debate is that both forces are important and interactive. Advances in basic knowledge make possible exploitation of opportunities for profit while profit opportunities stimulate research. ... Markets affording some opportunity for realizing monopoly profits through invention, and in which incumbent firms' profits are vulnerable to erosion through innovation by others, appear to be the ones with the greatest level of innovative activity."

   Kamien and Schwartz, supra note 1 at 217-18.

7. Kamien and Schwartz, supra note 1 at 142.

8. Kamien and Schwartz, supra note 1 at 216-17.

9. Machlup, supra note 5 at 175-76. Scherer notes that firms may innovate even without patent protection where there are (1) natural imitation lags, e.g. from the time it takes to gain necessary know-how, (2) the "advantages of competitive product leadership", e.g., the product differentiation advantage of being first or (3) where there are market structure characteristics apart from patents which will inhibit rapid entry and imitation. F.M. Scherer, *Industrial Market Structure and Economic Performance*, 444-47 (2d ed. 1980).

10. *International Technology Licensing : Survey Results*, Table 40, OECD (1987).

11. Id., at 61-62.

12. F.J. Contractor, *International Technology Licensing: Compensation, Costs and Negotiation*, Table 4-4 (1981).

13. *Intellectual Property Rights*, supra note 1 at 28; *Intellectual Property and Innovation* 27 (Cmnd. 9712, 1986).

14. F.M. Scherer, supra note 4.

15. Id., at 216.

16. Id., at 207-08.

Chapter 3

1. It should also be pointed out that large profits are not necessarily objectional from the point of view of competition policy. Profit acts as an efficient signal to direct investment in a market economy. Competition policy, concerned with preventing concerted practices, mergers to gain market power and the abuse of dominant positions, can be seen as aimed at controlling practices the profits of which would serve to misdirect investment rather than to steer it efficiently.

2. International Salt Co. v. United States, 332 U.S. 392 (1947). See generally, L.A. Sullivan, *Antitrust Law*, 434-37 (1977); W. Montgomery, *The Presumption of Economic Power for Patented and Copyrighted Products in Tying Arrangements*, 85 Columbia L. Rev. 1140 , notes 9-26 and accompanying text. Montgomery points out, however, that International Salt, although later cited for this presumption, was actually decided before an express market power requirement was established in tying cases. Id.

3. United States v. Loew's, 371 U.S. 38 (1962). See also, Montgomery, supra note 2. But see Title II of the Patent and Trademark Office Authorisation Act, Pub. L. No. 100-703 (1988) (patent misuse cannot be found on the basis of an alleged tie-in arrangement unless the patent owner has market power in the relevant market for the "tying" patent or patented product and any anticompetitive effect of the tie-in is not outweighed by the benefits of the arrangement, including procompetitive benefits and other business justifications). See also US Department of Justice Antitrust Division *Antitrust Enforcement Guidelines for International Operations* (Nov. 10, 1988) (hereinafter "*DOJ Guidelines*").

4. W.S. Bowman, *Patent and Antitrust Law*, 62, 65 (1973).

5. R.A. Posner, *Antitrust Law, An Economic Perspective*, 172 note 3 (1976).

6. V. Korah, *Exclusive Licences of Patent and Plant Breeders' Rights under EEC Law after Maize Seed* 28 Antitrust Bulletin 699,708 (1983); W.S. Bowman, supra note 4 at 53; F.M. Scherer, *Industrial Market Structure and Economic Performance*, 440 (2d ed. 1980).

7. F.J. Contractor, *International Technology Licensing: Compensation, Costs and Negotiations*, Table 5-7 (1981).

8. Id. at 115.

9. M.J. Meurer, *An Economic Analysis of Royalty Terms in Patent Licenses*, 67 Minnesota L. Rev 1198, note 5 (1983), citing Hammond and Medlock, *Lessons Learned from Recent Licensing Cases*, in 2 Technology Licensing 171 (T. Arnold and T. Smegal eds. 1982); W. Montgomery, supra note 2 at notes 64-68 and accompanying text.

10. See, e.g., Posner, supra note 5 at 171-74; Bowman, supra note 4 at 55, 104; Wollenberg, *An Economic Analysis of Tie-In Sales: Re-examining the Leverage Theory*, 39 Stanford L. Rev. 737 (1987); J.G. Sidak, *Debunking Predatory Innovation* 83 Columbia L. Rev. 1121; Meurer, supra note 9 at 140-145; W.R. Cornish, *Intellectual Property: Patents, Copyright, Trade Marks and Allied Rights*, 242 (1981). Cf, Scherer, supra note 6 at 582; J. Franco, *Limiting the Anticompetitive Prerogative of Patent Owners; Predatory Standards in Patent Licensing* 92 Yale L. Journal 831 (1983) (While the leveraging theory has been severely criticized, perpetuation of market power may occur by refusing to licence); L. Kaplow, *Extension of Monopoly Power Through Leverage* 85 Columbia L. Rev. 515 (1985). Kaplow argues in part that the critics of leveraging employ static analysis, while the conduct may be dynamic. Id. at notes 58-63 and accompanying text.

11. See, e.g., Bowman, supra note 4 at 61, 138-39, 240-41.

12. *Predatory Pricing*, OECD (1989).

13. E.g., W.O. Lavey, *Patents, Copyrights and Trademarks as Sources of Market Power in Antitrust Cases*, 27 Antitrust Bulletin 433, 436-38 (1982); R.B. Andewelt, *Analysis of Patent Pools under the Antitrust Laws*, 53 Antitrust L. Journal 611, 625 (1984).

14. See, e.g., Posner, supra note 5 at 173; Bork, *The Antitrust Paradox*, 373 (1978); Cornish, supra note 10 at 242; F.H. Easterbrook, *Vertical Arrangements and the Rule of Reason*, 53 Antitrust L. Journal 133, 143-44 (1984).

15. See, e.g., Sidak, supra note 10 at 1130-32.

16. See, e.g., Bork, supra note 14 at 372-78 (using the example of film rentals); Bowman supra note 4 at 116-18.

17. Cornish argues that to invalidate a term in a licence agreement one should show how that term reduces competition beyond the monopoly granted by the patent. Cornish, supra note 10 at 234.

18. Note that the gain to productive efficiency through licensing depends to some extent on the nature of the patent laws in a particular jurisdiction. In those jurisdictions where a patentee is under no obligation to practise his patent, putting a patent to work through licensing represents a clear gain to society. In other jurisdictions the situation is a bit less clear as compulsory licensing is available for non-working, at least in theory.

19. See, e.g., H. Hovenkamp, *Antitrust Policy after Chicago*, 84 Michigan L. Rev. 213 (1985), for a recent summary of the debate.

20. Note that profit-maximization is legitimate only for the appropriation of the consumer surplus generated by the innovation and different considerations apply to profits generated by cartel agreements between horizontal competitors or by agreements which increase the market power of the firms involved.

21. See, e.g. Sidak, supra note 10 at 1132.

22. R. Bork, supra note 14 at 395-97 (citing J. Robinson, *The Economics of Imperfect Competition*, 188-95 (1st Ed. 1933)).

23. Baxter, for example has expressed the analysis as follows:
"To the extent the monopolist is able to segregate his customers, he maximizes his returns by selling to each segment of the market that quantity of product necessary to make the marginal revenue in each segment equal to the marginal cost of the entire output. More generally stated, the discriminating monopolist continues to regard his supply (cost) situation as a single, aggregate function: but he calculates separate demand and marginal revenue curves for each of the segregated submarkets and disregards the aggregate demand curve which the sum of the submarkets would yield. He then notes the price and output in each submarket at which the marginal revenue curve in that submarket equals marginal cost of total output; and in each submarket he offers the indicated portion of output at the indicated price. Since the marginal revenue curve will lie farther below the demand curve in submarkets with less elastic demand than in those with more elastic demand, the consequence will be to offer lower quantities at higher prices in less elastic submarkets and larger quantities at lower prices in more elastic submarkets than would be appropriate if a uniform price were charged. Revenue will be increased and consumer surplus will be decreased. ... The effect on aggregate output is less certain: it depends, obviously, on whether the increased sales in more elastic markets exceed, equal or are exceeded by the decreased sales in less elastic markets. Because output is necessarily greater under perfect discrimination than under single-price monopoly, it might be supposed on intuitive grounds that each additional subdivision of markets approached that end position and would result in some increase in output. But the assumption is false; the effect on aggregate output will depend on the comparative rates of change of elasticity in the demand curves of the several segregated markets over those price ranges involved in the shift from uniform to discriminatory pricing. Output will increase if demand in the favoured market is becoming more elastic faster than demand in the disfavoured market is becoming inelastic; it will decrease if these conditions are reversed."

W. Baxter, *Legal Restrictions on Exploitation of the Patent Monopoly: An Economic Analysis*, 76 Yale L. Journal 267, 369-70 (1966).

24. J. Robinson, *The Economics of Imperfect Competition*, 201-202 (1933).

25. E.g., in the Monopolies and Mergers Commission report on the practices of Rank Xerox, the Commission exonerated certain pricing practices, which included charging both for the basic rental of the machine and a metered charge per copy. A second practice discriminated between those whose copies were made in long runs and those who made fewer at a time but with the same total number of copies. The MMC's report on these practices stated:

> "We do not think that the forms of price discrimination practised by Rank Xerox, as described above, are or have been against the public interest. If Rank Xerox had charged the same fixed rent to all customers, together with a small variable charge to cover the costs of servicing and supplies, the fixed rent would almost certainly have been pitched at a level which would have made Rank Xerox machines too expensive for less intensive users. The spread of the use of plain paper copiers would have been slower and the competitive impact of the technological innovation on the market for copying would have been reduced. Similarly, under a scheme of charging that did not discriminate according to the different uses of a machine but prescribed a uniform charge per copy, users of hired machines would not so effectively have exploited the versatility of the machines as under the system actually used.
>
> The discrimination resulting from the rental system might be objectionable if it served to inhibit competition. The standard rental terms relate to single machines, and we are satisfied that they do not inhibit competition. For example, an efficient competitor producing a machine similar to a Rank Xerox machine could match the company's standard rental scheme even if it produced far fewer machines and a more limited range of models than Rank Xerox. Further there is no evidence that under the Standard Commercial Terms any category of user or of use of rented machines has been unprofitable to Rank Xerox; that is, there is no evidence that any category of user or of use has been subsidised, thereby undermining the competition of other suppliers. We conclude that Rank Xerox's pricing policy, in so far as it relates to individual machines, does not operate against the public interest. This conclusion relates both to the gradation of charges with a monthly copy volume per machine and also to the modal system of charging."

Mergers and Monopolies Commission, *Indirect Electrostatic Reprographic Equipment* p. 97 (1976).

26. Bowman, supra note 4 at 55-56; Wollenberg, supra note 10 at notes 89-93 and accompanying text.

27. Bork, supra note 14 at 397.

28. Bowman, supra note 4 at 111-12.

29. P. Demaret, *Patents Territorial Restrictions and EEC Law: A Legal and Economic Analysis*, 45,124 (1978).

30. R.A. Posner, supra note 5 at 147-51; F.M. Scherer, *The Economics of Vertical Restraints* 52 Antitrust L. Journal 687, text accompanying notes 10-11 (1983). Note, however, that Scherer goes on to question the frequency with which such activity occurs. See also, Korah, supra note 4.

31. Scherer, supra note 30 at note 14.

32. Id., Scherer questions how serious the free rider problem is in practice but finds that it is most likely to occur in the sale of complex items. He further cautions that service competition created by vertical restrictions may reduce rather than increase efficiency to the extent that the practice becomes widespread and low cost/low service options are eliminated. Id. at text accompanying note 26.

33. See, e.g., Sidak, supra note 10 at 1135. compare Korah, supra note 6 (using the example of exclusive licences).

34. Wallenberg, supra note 10 at text accompanying notes 115-119.

35. Id.

36. Sidak, supra note 10 at 1135 note 46.

37. R.A. Klitzke, *Patents and Section 7 of the Clayton Act: The Significance of Patents in Corporate Acquisitions*, 1982 Intellectual Property Law Review 439, 451-53.

38. Id.

39. See, e.g., DOJ *Guidelines*, supra note 3, at Case 11.

40. Id.

41. Andewelt, supra note 13 at 615-16.

42. V. Korah, *Monopolies and Restrictive Practices* 133 (1968).

43. Andewelt, supra note 13 at 616.

44. Id.

45. See, e.g., Bork, supra note 14 at 379-80; Sidak, supra note 10 at 1136-37.

46. Sidak, supra note 10 at 1136-37.

47. See, e.g., Posner, supra note 5 at 175-76.

48. Bowman, supra note 4 at 76-88.

49. Id.

50. Id. at 91-92.

51. Andewelt, supra note 13 at 618.

52. Korah, supra note 42 at 133; Andewelt, supra note 13 at 621-29.

53. Demaret, supra note 29 at 46.

54. See, e.g., DOJ *Guidelines* supra note 3 at Section 3.62, n. 131.

55. J.S. Venit, *Know-How Licensing under EEC Law: Where We Have Been, Where We Are, and Where We May Be Headed* 32 Antitrust Bulletin 189, 218 (1987).

56. R.B. Andewelt, *Basic Principle to Apply at Patent Antitrust Interface*, (Remarks before the Houston Texas Patent Law Association, Dec. 3, 1981).

57. Andewelt, supra note 13 at 617.

58. Scherer, supra note 30; J.T. Halverson, *Vertical Restraints After GTE Sylvania: Current Confusions: An Overview of Legal and Economic Issues and the Relevance of the Vertical Restraints Guide*, 52 Antitrust L. Journal 49 (1983).

59. Easterbrook, supra note 14 at 141-42.

60. Scherer, supra note 30; Halverson, supra note 58.

61. See, e.g., Easterbrook, supra note 14 at 161-62.

62. See, e.g., Easterbrook, supra note 14 at note 22. [Citing Peterman, *The International Salt Case*, 22 Journal of Law and Economics 351 (1979)].

63. T.G. Krattenmaker and S.L. Salop, *Anticompetitive Exclusion: Raising Rivals' Costs to Achieve Power over Price*, 96 Yale Law Journal at 234-55 (1986).

64. Paras. 25-26, supra.

65. See generally, Andewelt, supra note 13.

66. See, e.g., DOJ *Guidelines*, supra note 3, at Section 3.65.

67. Andewelt, supra note 13 at 624-25.

68. See, e.g., Bork, supra note 14 at 155-60, 347-48. This is distinct from the problem of a firm seeking to use the courts to enforce an invalid patent. See, e.g., R.J. Hoerner, *Bad Faith Enforcement of Patents - Antitrust Considerations*, 55 Antitrust L. Journal 421 (1986).

Chapter 4

1. Patent Law of 28th March, 1984, Article 45, Sections 1, 4, 5.

2. Id. at Section 6.

3. Id. at Article 50, Section 2.

4. Senat de Belgique, *Exposé des motifs, projet de loi sur la protection contre l'abus de la puissance économique* (Session de 1957-58, 19 novembre 1957).

5. Id. at 14-18.

6. See Statute No. 102 of 31st March 1955 on supervision of monopolies and restrictive practices as amended - Consolidation Act No. 108 of 11th March 1986 - (The Monopolies Act), Section 1, Section 2, Subsection 1, Section 6 and Section 10.

7. Id.

8. See the Monopolies Act, Section 11, Subsection 2, and Statute No. 59 of 15th February 1974 on prices and profits as amended - Consolidation Act No. 109 of 11th March 1986 - (The Prices and Profits Act), Section 7, Subsection 1.

9. See The Monopolies Act, Section 12, and the Prices and Profits Act, Section 6.

10. See "Den kommenterede patentlov", 2nd edition (The Patents Act - annotated edition), Juristforbundets Forlag, Copenhagen 1979, page 246 f (not available in English).

11. See "Betenkning angaende Nordisk Patentlovgivning, Nordisk Utredningsserie 1963:6", February 1964, p. 109 (not available in English).

12. See Mogens Koktvedgaard: "Immaterialretspositioner" (Legal Positions of Incorporeal Rights), Juristforbundets Forlag, Copenhagen 1965, p. 39-40 (summary in English).

13. See the MCA's "Rapport om laegemiddelbranchen - struktur, konkurrence og priser", Copenhagen 1978 (not available in English).

14. Cf. the Patent Law of 2nd January 1968 as modified by the laws of 13th July 1978 and 11th June 1970 concerning protected plant varieties.

15. Articles 32 and 33 of the law of 2nd January 1968 provide for compulsory licenses in the case of non-use given the public interest in seeing patents exploited. A patentee may be subject to compulsory licensing if he has not at least made serious preparations for exploitation with three years of the granting of a patent or four years of filing.

16. The holder of an improvements patent may seek the compulsory licensing of a blocking patent under Article 36 of the Patent law, which may be granted under the same terms as a licence for non-use. Likewise, the holder of the blocking patent may seek a compulsory licence of the improvements patent.

17. A licence of right may be granted under Articles 37-40 of the Patent Law under a ministerial order which also fixes the terms of the licence. Failing agreement, royalties are fixed by the High Court (*Tribunal de Grande Instance*). Licences as of right may be granted in the following situations:

    Public health (Article 37) may require a licence for a pharmaceutical-related patent where the patented product is produced in insufficient quantity or quality or is sold at an excessively high price, thus permitting the control of an abuse of dominant position.

    National Economic Interests (Article 39) may give rise to a licence of right of any non-health related patent by a decree of the Conseil d'Etat where non-use is harmful to economic development and the public interest.

    National Defence (Article 40) may also be the basis for a licence of right.

    Apart from patents, licences of right may also be provided in the case of protected plant varieties under Articles 12 and 15 of the Law of 11th June 1970.

18. Phytosanitaires, Chapter 5 infra at note 1.

19. DL no. 422/83 of 3rd December 1983.

20. Article 2 part 5, Royal Decree 1750/87 of 18th December 1987.

21. Cf. Govt Bill 1953: 103 p. 227 f.

22. Govt Bill 1960: 167 p. 37, 1966: 40 p. 179, 1969: 168 p. 52 and 338.

23. MD 1972: 7, PKF 1972: 5

24. See Govt Bill 1977/78 Part A p. 330 f, SOU 1978:9 p. 264 f, Govt Bill 1981/82:165 p. 194.

25. See Bernitz in NIR 1973 p. 1 ff. See also, NIR 1982 p. 444 ff, Bernitz et al, Immaterialratt, Stockholm 1983, p. 178, Bernitz, Svensk marknadsratt, Uddevalla 1986, p. 98.

26. SOU 1978:9.

27. Id. at p. 141 ff.

28. 1977 All ER 47.

29. Office of Fair Trading, *Anticompetitive Practices: A Guide to the Provisions of the Competition Act 1980* (1986) at 14.

30. Department of Trade and Industry, *Intellectual Property and Innovation* (Cmnd 9712, 1986) at 27.

31. See, e.g., International Salt Co. v. United States, 332 US 392, 396 (1947). See also, Jefferson Parish Hospital Dist. No. 2 v. Hyde, 466 US 2 (1984).

32. See Loctite Corp. v. Ultra Seal Ltd. 781 F 2d 861, note 9 (Fed. Cir. 1985).

33. Walker Process Equipmpent v. Food Machinery and Chemical Corp., 382 US 172 (1965).

34. Id. at 177.

35. *Jefferson Parish*, 466 US at 16.

36. Id. at 37, note 7.

37. See, e.g. Henry v. A.B. Dick Co., 224 US 1, 28-29 (1911).

38. See, 35 U.S.C. Section 261.

39. See, e.g., United States v. General Electric 272 US 476, 488-89 (1926).

40. See generally, R.J. Hoerner, *Patent Misuse*, 53 Antitrust Law Journal 641, (1984).

41. Under Section 3105 of the Act, conduct which: "(1) licensed the patent under terms that affect commerce outside the scope of the patent's claims, (2) restricted a licensee of the patent in the sale of the patented product or in the sale of a product made by the patented process, (3) obligated a licensee of the patent to pay royalties that differ from those paid by another licensee or that are allegedly excessive, (4) obligated a licensee of the patent to pay royalties in amounts not related to the licensee's sales of the patented product or a product made by the patented process, (5) refused to license the patent to any person, or (6) otherwise used the patent allegedly to suppress competition", would not be grounds for patent misuse unless it independently violated the antitrust laws.

42. US Department of Justice, *Vertical Restraints Guidelines* (1985) at Section 2.4.

43. US Department of Justice, Antitrust Division, *Antitrust Enforcement Guidelines for International Operations*, (Nov. 10, 1988) (hereinafter "*DOJ Guidelines*").

44. Id. at Section 3.6 See C.F. Rule, *The Antitrust Implications of International Licensing: After the Nine No-No's,* reprinted in 4 Trade Reg. Rep. (CCH) Section 13,131 (1986).

45. Id. at Section 3.61. See C.F. Rule, *The Administration's Views: Antitrust Analysis After the Nine No-No's*, 55 Antitrust L.J. 365 (1986).

46. *DOJ Guidelines* at Section 3.66

47. Id.

48. Id. at Section 3.62.

49. See, e.g., Centrafarm BV v. Sterling Drug Inc., Case 15:74, 1974 E.C.R.1147.

50. Commission Regulation No 2349/84, 23 July 1984, OJ No. L.219/15, 16th August 1984.

51. OJ No L 61, 4th March 1989.

52. Id. at Article 1(7). The terms "secret", "substantial" and "identified" are further defined as follows:

   "(2) The term 'secret' means that the know-how package as a body or in the precise configuration and assembly of its components is not generally known or easily accessible, so that part of its value consists in the lead-time the licensee gains when it is communicated to him; it is not limited to the narrow sense that each individual component of the know-how should be totally unknown or unobtainable outside the licensor's business.

   (3) The term 'substantial' means that the know-how includes information which is of importance for the whole or a significant part of (i) a manufacturing process or (ii) a product or service, or (iii) for the development thereof and excludes information which is trivial. Such know-how must thus be useful, i.e. can reasonably be expected at the date of conclusion of the agreement to be capable of improving the competitive position of the licensee, for example by helping him to enter a new market or giving him an advantage in competition with other manufacturers or providers of services who do not have access to the licensed secret know-how or other comparable secret know-how.

   (4) The term 'identified' means know-how defined or recorded in such a manner as to make it possible to verify that it fulfils the criteria of secrecy and substantiality and to ensure that the licensee is not unduly restricted in his exploitation of his own technology. To be identified the know-how can either be set out in the licence agreement or in a separate document or recorded in any other appropriate form by the latest at the time the know-how is transferred or shortly thereafter, provided that the separate document or other record can be made available if the need arises."

   Id.

Chapter 5

1. Phytosanitaires, reported in Lamy, *Jurisprudence*, No. 213 (26th May 1983).

2. BGH, Decision of 15th March 1973, WuW 9/1973, 643.

3. NO Log nr 260/75, PKF 1976:5, p.58.

4. United States v. General Electric Co., 272 US 476 (1926).

5. Id. at 484, 494. Resale price maintenance was by that time per se unlawful under the doctrine of Dr. Miles Medical Co. v. John D. Park and Sons, 220 US 373 (1911), which involved efforts to set the resale price of unpatented but secret proprietary medicines. Further, rights in a patented item were by then long considered to be exhausted on the first sale. *General Electric*, 272 US at 489.

6. Id. at 489.

7. Id. at 490.

8. Id.

9. United States v. Univis Lens Co., 316 US 241 (1941).

10. United States v. Line Material Co., 333 US 287 (1947).
11. Id. at 314.
12. United States v. United States Gypsum Co., 333 US 364 (1947).
13. Id. at 391.
14. Monsanto Co. v. Spray Rite Service Co., 465 US 752 (1984).
15. Business Electronics Corp. v. Sharp Electronics Corp. 56 U.S.L.W. 4387 (May 2, 1988).
16. Continental TV Inc. v. GTE Sylvania Inc. 433 US 36 (1977).
17. *Monsanto*, 465 US at 462-63.
18. In particular, the Court noted that vertical price fixing can facilitate the maintenance of a cartel at either the manufacturer or retailer level. Slip. op. at 16.
19. Slip op. at 18.
20. OJ No. L 219/15 (16th August 1984).
21. Id. at Article 3(6).
22. OJ No. L 61, 4th March 1989, at Article 3(8).
23. Casiers à bouteilles, reported in Lamy, *Jurisprudence*, No. 84 (17th March 1981).
24. Q-Tips Inc. v. Johnson and Johnson, 109 F. Supp 657 (D.N.J. 1951).
25. Patent Exemption, supra note 20 at Article 3(5).
26. Know-how Exemption, supra note 22 at Articles 3(7) and 4(2).
27. ENI/Montedison, OJ No. L 5/13 (7th January 1987).
28. See NO log no: 211/75. PKF 1979: 1 p. 89.
29. NO log no: 330/76, PKF 1976: 10 p. 49.
30. NO log no: 421/85.
31. 35 U.S.C. Section 261. See also, Ethyl Gasoline Corp. v. United States 309 US 436 (1940).
32. *GTE Sylvania*, 433 US at 54-55 (citations omitted).
33. Id. at 54.
34. Id. at 56.
35. Dunlop Co. v. Kelsey-Hayes Co., 484 F.2d 407 (6th Cir. 1973).
36. United States v. Westinghouse Elec. Corp., 648 US 642 (9th cir. 1981).
37. Id. at 647.
38. Id. at 648.
39. DOJ Guidelines at Case 12.
40. Id.
41. Centrafarm BV v. Sterling Drug Inc., Case 15/74, 1974 E.C.R. 1147.
42. Id. at 1162-63.
43. Burroughs/Geha-Werke, OJ L 13/53 (17th January 1972).
44. Burroughs/Delplanque, OJ L 13/50 (17th January 1972).
45. Raymond/Nagoya, OJ L 143/39 (23rd June 1972).
46. Kabelmetal/Luchaire, OJ No. L 222/34 (22nd August 1975).
47. Nungesser v. Commission, Case 258/78, 1982 E.C.R. 2015.
48. Id. at 2063.
49. Id. at 2065.

50. Id. at 2070.

51. Id. at 2070-71.

52. Id. at 2072-74.

53. Patent Exemption, supra note 20 at article 1(1)(1-2).

54. Id. at article 1(1)(3).

55. Id. at article 1(1)(4).

56. Id. at article 1(1)(5).

57. Id. at article 1(1)(4).

58. Id. at article 1(1)(5).

59. Id. at article 3(11).

60. Boussois/Interpane, OJ No. 13/204 (15th December 1986).

61. Know-how Exemption, supra note 22 at Articles 1(1) and (2).

62. Transfield Pty. Ltd. v. Arlo International Ltd., ATPR pp. 40-166 (1980).

63. See "Meddelelser fra Monopoltilsynet - 1963", Copenhagen 1964, p. 55-56 (not available in English).

64. Fil-Mousse, reported in Lamy, *Jurisprudence*, No. 35 (22nd June 1962).

65. BGH, Decision of 25th October 1966, WuW 10/1967, 681.

66. BGH, Decision of 5th May 1967, WuW 10/1967, 696.

67. BGH, Decision of 14th October 1976, WuW 5/1977, 338.

68. BGH, Decision of 13th March 1979, WuW 11/1979, 752.

69. NO log no: 6/77, PKF 1979: 6 pp 68 et seq.

70. 35 USC Section 261.

71. National Lockwasher Co. v. George K. Garrett Co., 137 F. 2d 255 (3rd cir. 1943).

72. Id.

73. Jefferson Parish Hospital Dist. No. 2 v. Hyde, 466 US 2 (1984).

74. Id. at 45.

75. DOJ Guidelines at Case 10, page 66.

76. Id.

77. Chapter 4 supra at text accompanying note 48.

78. Id.

79. Id.

80. See, e.g., AOIP/Beyrard, OJ No. L 6/8 (13th January 1976), where the Commission stated: "By clause 1(1) the licensor grants to the licensee the exclusive right to manufacture and sell the patented devices in France and in the countries of the former French Union. This clause has, as its object and effect, a restriction of competition in that, by granting to a single firm the right to exploit his monopoly in a given territory, the licensor gives up for the duration of the agreement the power to grant in respect of the same territory licences to other firms, thus preventing competition from arising in the present case between several licenses. This is an appreciable restriction of competiion in view of the size of the licensee's turnover in respect of the patented devices, and of its market share in France and in certain other Member States of the EEC". Id. at 12.
Similar reasoning can be found, e.g. in Kablemetal-Luchaire, supra note 46 at 37 and Burroughs-Geha Werke, supra note 43.

81. See, e.g. Kabelmetal/Luchaine, supra note 46 at 38.

82. Nungesser v. Commission, supra note 47 at 2065-69.

83. Patent Exemption, supra note 20 at Article 1(1)(1-2).

84. Id. at article 3(3).

85. Interpane Boussois, supra note 60.

86. Id.

87. Know-how Exemption, supra note 22 at Article 1(1) and (2).

88. Id. at Article 3(11).

89. Id. at Article 3(9).

90. Id.

91. Magnésium, reported in Lamy, *Jurisprudence*, No. 3 (8th October 1955).

92. General Talking Pictures v. Western Electric Co., 304 US 175 (1937), *aff'd on rehearing* 305 US 124 (1938).

93. Id. at 181.

94. United States v. Studiengesellschaft Kohle m.b.H., 670 F. 2d 1122 (D.C. Cir. 1981).

95. Id. at 1129-30.

96. Id. at 1136.

97. Id.

98. Patent Exemption, supra note 20 at Article 2(1)(3), Know-how Exemption, supra note 22 at Article 2(1)(10).

99. Id.

100. NO log no: 186/81, POK 1983: 2 pp 67 et seq; 1985: 402; 1987: 64.

101. Sidney Henry v. A.B. Dick Co., 244 U.S. I (1911).

102. Motion Picture Patents Co. v. Universal Film Manufacturing Co., 243 US 502 (1916).

103. Id. at 517-18.

104. Morton Salt Co. v. G.S. Suppinger Co. 314 US 488 (1941).

105. B.B. Chemical v. Ellis, 314 US 495 (1941).

106. Mercoid Corp. v. Mid-Continent Investment Co., 320 US 661 (1943).

107. Mercoid Corp. v. Minneapolis Honeywell Regulator Co., 320 US 680 (1943).

108. See 320 US 680, 682-83.

109. 320 US 661, 666-67 (Citations omitted).

110. International Salt Co. v. United States, 332 US 392 (1947).

111. Id.

112. Id.

113. Dawson Chemical Co. v. Rohm and Haas Co., 448 US 176 (1980).

114. Id. at 221-22.

115. Jefferson Parish Hospital Dist. No. 2 v. Hyde, 466 US 2 (1984).

116. Id. at 14-15 and note 23.

117. Id. at 15-17.

118. Id. at 16.

119. Id. at 37-39.

120. Id. at 41.

121. Id. at 36 note 4.

122. Id. at 37 note 7.

123. Vaessen/Morris, OJ No L 19/32 (26th January 1979).

124. Id. at 35.

125. Id. at 36.

126. Automatic Radio Mfg. Co. v. Hazeltine Research Inc., 339 US 827 (1950).

127. American Securit Co. v. Shatterproof Glass Corp., 268 F. 2d 769 (3d Cir. 1959).

128. Id. at 777.

129. Western Electric Co. v. Stewart Warner Corp. 631 F. 2d 333 (4th Cir. 1980).

130. BGH, Decision of 16th October 1962, WuW 10/1963, 815.

131. Bundeskartellamt, Decision of 30th September 1981, WuW 2/1982, 149.

132. Automatic Radio Mfg Co. v. Hazeltine Research, Inc. 339 US 827 (1950).

133. Id. at 834.

134. Zenith Radio Corp. v. Hazeltine Research Inc. 395 US 100 (1969).

135. Id. at 139.

136. Brulotte v. Thys Co. 379 US 29 (1964).

137. Id. at 32.

138. Id. at 34-39.

139. Rockform Corp. v. Acitelli-Standard Concrete Wall Inc., 367 F 2d 678 (6th Cir. 1966).

140. Id. at 680-81.

141. Beckman Instruments Inc. v. Technical Development Corp. 433 F 2d 55 (7th Cir. 1970).

142. Id. at 60-61.

143. Miller Insituform v. Insituform or North America, 605 F Supp 1125 (M.D. Term. 1985).

144. Id. at 1133-34.

145. DOJ Guidelines at Case 10, page 66.

146. AOIP/Beyrard, OJ No. L 6/8 (13th January 1976).

147. Id. at 13.

148. Transparent-Wrap Machine Corp. v. Stokes and Smith Co. 329 US 637 (1946).

149. Id. at 646-47 (citation omitted).

150. Id. at 642, 648.

151. DOJ Guidelines at Case 11, page 71.

152. Raymond/Nagoya, supra note 45.

153. Kabelmetal/Luchaire, supra note 46.

154. Id. at 37-38.

155. Lear v. Adkins, 395 US 653 (1969).

156. Id. at 670.

157. Id.

158. Vaessen/Morris at 34-35.

159. Id.

160. Raymond/Nagoya, supra note 45.

161. Bayer/Süllhöfer, Case 65/86, decided 27th September 1988.

162. Standard Oil Co. v. United States, 283 US 163 (1930).

163. Id. at 175.

164. Id. at 171 (citation omitted).

165. Hartford-Empire Co. v. United States, 323 US 386 (1945).

166. Id. at note 53a.

167. DOJ Guidelines at Case 11, page 68.

168. Id.

169. Semences, céréales à paille, maïs et endives, reported in Lamy, *Jurisprudence*, No. 252 (10th October 1985).

170. Monopolies and Mergers Commission, *The Supply of Indirect Electrostatic Reprographic Equipment* (December 1976).

171. See Chapter 3, note 30 supra.

172. Under Section 51 of the Patents Act 1977, a Minister may seek compulsory licensing of a patent following a report by the MMC under the Fair Trade Act 1973 that there is a patent-related monopoly situation operating against the public interest. Later amendments also provide for compulsory licensing of a MMC report under the Competition Act 1980. Under either Act, the Comptroller-General of Patents, Designs and Trade Marks may order compulsory licensing at a reasonable royalty if he finds either restrictive patent licensing or a refusal to license.

173. Monopolies and Mergers Commission, *Ford Motor Co. Ltd* (February 1985).

174. While Ford's position had been that 60 per cent was an appropriate rate, the undertaking provides for a royalty of only two per cent of the sales price of the parts. The undertaking requires Ford to license crash parts once a car has been on the market seven years.

175. British Leyland Motor Corp. v. Armstrong Patents Co. Ltd, (1986) 1 A.C. 577.

176. Bement v. National Harrow Co, 186 US.S 70 (1982).

177. Id.

178. Id., (citing Heaton Peninsular Co. v. Eureka Specialty Co., 47 U.S. App. 146, 160).

179. Xerox Corp., 86 FTC 364 (1975).

180. SCM Corp. v. Xerox Corp., 564 F rd 1195 (2d Cir. 1981).

181. Id. at 1206.

182. Id. at 1204.

183. United States v. Westinghouse, 648 F. 2d 642 (9th Cir. 1981).

184. E.I. Dupont de Nemours & Co, 96 FTC 653 (1980).

185. Id. at 748 (footnote omitted).

186. Volvo/Veng, Case 238/87, decided 5th October 1988.

WHERE TO OBTAIN OECD PUBLICATIONS
OÙ OBTENIR LES PUBLICATIONS DE L'OCDE

ARGENTINA - ARGENTINE
Carlos Hirsch S.R.L.,
Florida 165, 4° Piso,
(Galeria Guemes) 1333 Buenos Aires
Tel. 33.1787.2391 y 30.7122

AUSTRALIA - AUSTRALIE
D.A. Book (Aust.) Pty. Ltd.
11-13 Station Street (P.O. Box 163)
Mitcham, Vic. 3132   Tel. (03) 873 4411

AUSTRIA - AUTRICHE
OECD Publications and Information Centre,
4 Simrockstrasse,
5300 Bonn (Germany)   Tel. (0228) 21.60.45
Gerold & Co., Graben 31, Wien I Tel. 52.22.35

BELGIUM - BELGIQUE
Jean de Lannoy,
Avenue du Roi 202
B-1060 Bruxelles   Tel. (02) 538.51.69

CANADA
Renouf Publishing Company Ltd
1294 Algoma Road, Ottawa, Ont. K1B 3W8
Tel: (613) 741-4333
Stores:
61 rue Sparks St., Ottawa, Ont. K1P 5R1
Tel: (613) 238-8985
211 rue Yonge St., Toronto, Ont. M5B 1M4
Tel: (416) 363-3171
Federal Publications Inc.,
301-303 King St. W.,
Toronto, Ont. M5V 1J5   Tel. (416)581-1552
Les Éditions la Liberté inc.,
3020 Chemin Sainte-Foy,
Sainte-Foy, P.Q. G1X 3V6,   Tel. (418)658-3763

DENMARK - DANEMARK
Munksgaard Export and Subscription Service
35, Nørre Søgade, DK-1370 København K
Tel. +45.1.12.85.70

FINLAND - FINLANDE
Akateeminen Kirjakauppa,
Keskuskatu 1, 00100 Helsinki 10   Tel. 0.12141

FRANCE
OCDE/OECD
Mail Orders/Commandes par correspondance :
2, rue André-Pascal,
75775 Paris Cedex 16   Tel. (1) 45.24.82.00
Bookshop/Librairie : 33, rue Octave-Feuillet
75016 Paris
Tel. (1) 45.24.81.67 et/ou (1) 45.24.81.81
Librairie de l'Université,
12a, rue Nazareth,
13602 Aix-en-Provence   Tel. 42.26.18.08

GERMANY - ALLEMAGNE
OECD Publications and Information Centre,
4 Simrockstrasse,
5300 Bonn   Tel. (0228) 21.60.45

GREECE - GRÈCE
Librairie Kauffmann,
28, rue du Stade, 105 64 Athens Tel. 322.21.60

HONG KONG
Government Information Services,
Publications (Sales) Office,
Information Services Department
No. 1, Battery Path, Central

ICELAND - ISLANDE
Snæbjörn Jónsson & Co., h.f.,
Hafnarstræti 4 & 9,
P.O.B. 1131 – Reykjavik
Tel. 13133/14281/11936

INDIA - INDE
Oxford Book and Stationery Co.,
Scindia House, New Delhi 110001
Tel. 331.5896/5308
17 Park St., Calcutta 700016   Tel. 240832

INDONESIA - INDONÉSIE
Pdii-Lipi, P.O. Box 3065/JKT.Jakarta
Tel. 583467

IRELAND - IRLANDE
TDC Publishers - Library Suppliers,
12 North Frederick Street, Dublin 1
Tel. 744835-749677

ITALY - ITALIE
Libreria Commissionaria Sansoni,
Via Benedetto Fortini 120/10,
Casella Post. 552
50125 Firenze   Tel. 055/645415
Via Bartolini 29, 20155 Milano   Tel. 365083
La diffusione delle pubblicazioni OCSE viene
assicurata dalle principali librerie ed anche da :
Editrice e Libreria Herder,
Piazza Montecitorio 120, 00186 Roma
Tel. 6794628
Libreria Hœpli,
Via Hœpli 5, 20121 Milano   Tel. 865446
Libreria Scientifica
Dott. Lucio de Biasio "Aeiou"
Via Meravigli 16, 20123 Milano   Tel. 807679

JAPAN - JAPON
OECD Publications and Information Centre,
Landic Akasaka Bldg., 2-3-4 Akasaka,
Minato-ku, Tokyo 107   Tel. 586.2016

KOREA - CORÉE
Kyobo Book Centre Co. Ltd.
P.O.Box: Kwang Hwa Moon 1658,
Seoul   Tel. (REP) 730.78.91

LEBANON - LIBAN
Documenta Scientifica/Redico,
Edison Building, Bliss St.,
P.O.B. 5641, Beirut   Tel. 354429-344425

MALAYSIA/SINGAPORE -
MALAISIE/SINGAPOUR
University of Malaya Co-operative Bookshop
Ltd.,
7 Lrg 51A/227A, Petaling Jaya
Malaysia   Tel. 7565000/7565425
Information Publications Pte Ltd
Pei Fu Industrial Building,
24 New Industrial Road No. 02-06
Singapore 1953   Tel. 2831786, 2831798

NETHERLANDS - PAYS-BAS
SDU Uitgeverij
Christoffel Plantijnstraat 2
Postbus 20014
2500 EA's-Gravenhage   Tel. 070-789911
Voor bestellingen: Tel. 070-789880

NEW ZEALAND - NOUVELLE-ZÉLANDE
Government Printing Office Bookshops:
Auckland: Retail Bookshop, 25 Rutland Street,
Mail Orders, 85 Beach Road
Private Bag C.P.O.
Hamilton: Retail: Ward Street,
Mail Orders, P.O. Box 857
Wellington: Retail, Mulgrave Street, (Head
Office)
Cubacade World Trade Centre,
Mail Orders, Private Bag
Christchurch: Retail, 159 Hereford Street,
Mail Orders, Private Bag
Dunedin: Retail, Princes Street,
Mail Orders, P.O. Box 1104

NORWAY - NORVÈGE
Narvesen Info Center – NIC,
Bertrand Narvesens vei 2,
P.O.B. 6125 Etterstad, 0602 Oslo 6
Tel. (02) 67.83.10, (02) 68.40.20

PAKISTAN
Mirza Book Agency
65 Shahrah Quaid-E-Azam, Lahore 3 Tel. 66839

PHILIPPINES
I.J. Sagun Enterprises, Inc.
P.O. Box 4322 CPO Manila
Tel. 695-1946, 922-9495

PORTUGAL
Livraria Portugal, Rua do Carmo 70-74,
1117 Lisboa Codex   Tel. 360582/3

SINGAPORE/MALAYSIA -
SINGAPOUR/MALAISIE
See "Malaysia/Singapor". Voir
«Malaisie/Singapour»

SPAIN - ESPAGNE
Mundi-Prensa Libros, S.A.,
Castelló 37, Apartado 1223, Madrid-28001
Tel. 431.33.99
Libreria Bosch, Ronda Universidad 11,
Barcelona 7   Tel. 317.53.08/317.53.58

SWEDEN - SUÈDE
AB CE Fritzes Kungl. Hovbokhandel,
Box 16356, S 103 27 STH,
Regeringsgatan 12,
DS Stockholm   Tel. (08) 23.89.00
Subscription Agency/Abonnements:
Wennergren-Williams AB,
Box 30004, S104 25 Stockholm Tel. (08)54.12.00

SWITZERLAND - SUISSE
OECD Publications and Information Centre,
4 Simrockstrasse,
5300 Bonn (Germany)   Tel. (0228) 21.60.45
Librairie Payot,
6 rue Grenus, 1211 Genève 11
Tel. (022) 31.89.50
Maditec S.A.
Ch. des Palettes 4
1020 – Renens/Lausanne   Tel. (021) 635.08.65
United Nations Bookshop/Librairie des Nations-
Unies
Palais des Nations, 1211 – Geneva 10
Tel. 022-34-60-11 (ext. 48 72)

TAIWAN - FORMOSE
Good Faith Worldwide Int'l Co., Ltd.
9th floor, No. 118, Sec.2, Chung Hsiao E. Road
Taipei   Tel. 391.7396/391.7397

THAILAND - THAILANDE
Suksit Siam Co., Ltd., 1715 Rama IV Rd.,
Samyam Bangkok 5   Tel. 2511630
INDEX Book Promotion & Service Ltd.
59/6 Soi Lang Suan, Ploenchit Road
Patjumamwan, Bangkok 10500
Tel. 250-1919, 252-1066

TURKEY - TURQUIE
Kültur Yayinlari Is-Türk Ltd. Sti.
Atatürk Bulvari No: 191/Kat. 21
Kavaklidere/Ankara   Tel. 25.07.60
Dolmabahce Cad. No: 29
Besiktas/Istanbul   Tel. 160.71.88

UNITED KINGDOM - ROYAUME-UNI
H.M. Stationery Office,
Postal orders only: (01)873-8483
P.O.B. 276, London SW8 5DT
Telephone orders: (01) 873-9090, or
Personal callers:
49 High Holborn, London WC1V 6HB
Branches at: Belfast, Birmingham,
Bristol, Edinburgh, Manchester

UNITED STATES - ÉTATS-UNIS
OECD Publications and Information Centre,
2001 L Street, N.W., Suite 700,
Washington, D.C. 20036 - 4095
Tel. (202) 785.6323

VENEZUELA
Libreria del Este,
Avda F. Miranda 52, Aptdo. 60337,
Edificio Galipan, Caracas 106
Tel. 951.17.05/951.23.07/951.12.97

YUGOSLAVIA - YOUGOSLAVIE
Jugoslovenska Knjiga, Knez Mihajlova 2,
P.O.B. 36, Beograd   Tel. 621.992

Orders and inquiries from countries where
Distributors have not yet been appointed should be
sent to:
OECD, Publications Service, 2, rue André-Pascal,
75775 PARIS CEDEX 16.

Les commandes provenant de pays où l'OCDE n'a
pas encore désigné de distributeur doivent être
adressées à :
OCDE, Service des Publications. 2, rue André-
Pascal, 75775 PARIS CEDEX 16.

72380-1-1989

OECD PUBLICATIONS, 2, rue André-Pascal, 75775 PARIS CEDEX 16 - No. 44783 1989
PRINTED IN FRANCE
(24 89 03 1) ISBN 92-64-13242-2